HUNT VS. LAUDA: THE EPIC 1976 FORMULA 1 SEASON

HUNT VS. LAUDA

THE EPIC 1976 FORMULA 1 SEASON

PAUL FEARNLEY

DESIGN BY TOM MORGAN

DAVID BULL PUBLISHING

All photographs were generously provided by the L.A.T. Photographic archive in Teddington, UK.

Library of Congress Control Number: 2013939866

ISBN: 978 1 935007 19 7

David Bull Publishing, logo, and colophon are trademarks of David Bull Publishing, Inc.

Book and cover design: Tom Morgan, Blue Design, Portland, Maine

Printed in China

10 9 8 7 6 5 4 3 2 1

David Bull Publishing
4250 East Camelback Road
Suite K150
Phoenix, AZ 85018

602-852-9500
602-852-9503 (fax)

www.bullpublishing.com

Page 2: Roughhousing in the Kyalami pits. Lauda and Hunt were genuine friends. The 1976 season would test their bond to the limit before ultimately strengthening it. Quite why Ferrari appears to be assessing a full-wet Goodyear is a mystery, as it was warm and dry throughout the March weekend of the South African Grand Prix.

This page: The right result on the day—the first Englishman to win the British Grand Prix for 18 years. The restless crowd would go home happy, by which time the political machinations that would eventually rescind this Hunt "victory" were already well under way. Dig those flares! And that underwhelming singular row of Armco.

Page 6: James Hunt: British hero and heart-throb.

Page 8-9: The 1976 Formula 1 season gets off to a ragged start at the Brazilian Grand Prix. Front-row men Hunt (left) and Lauda lead the pack but are about to be overtaken by the latter's Ferrari teammate Clay Regazzoni. The cars at Interlagos were supposed to move forward from a dummy grid, pause in their correct position and wait to be released. Those towards the back, however, were given insufficient time to do so by an overeager official. Hence the big gaps in the field. F1 was still an inexact science.

CONTENTS

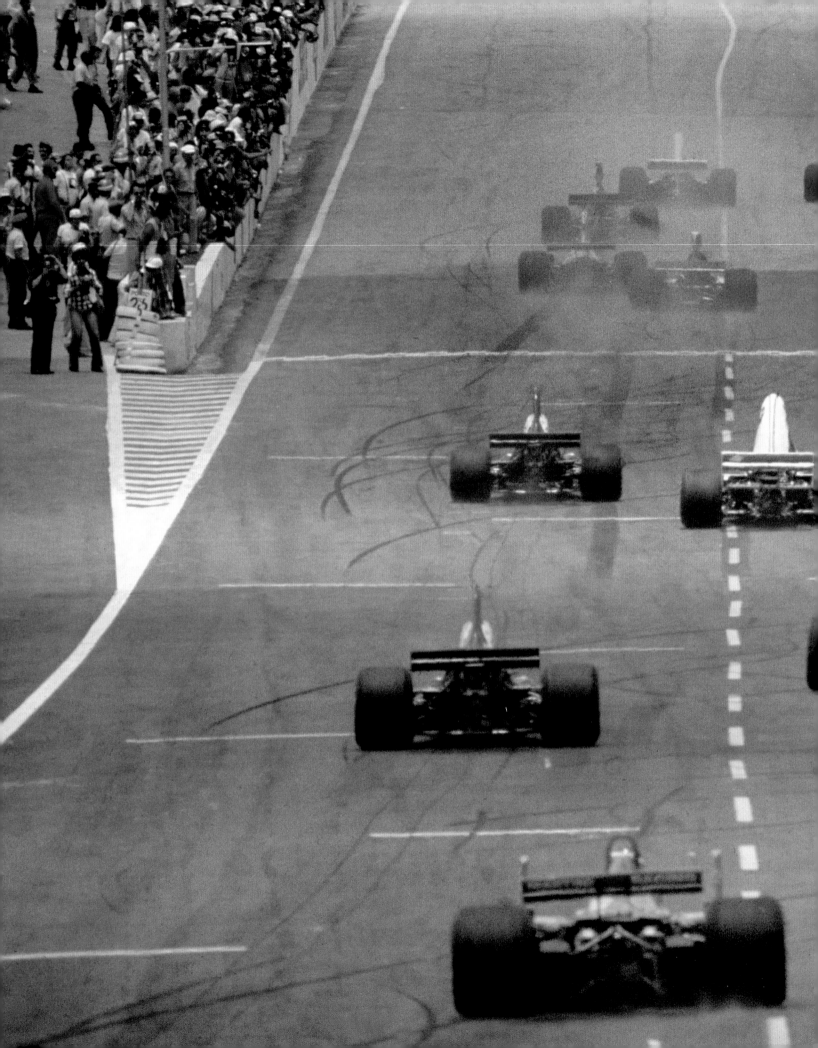

CHAPTER 1

Attraction of Opposites

Bucktoothed Niki Lauda had been called "The Rat" for years. Only after he had assumed Jackie Stewart's mantle as the thinking man's Formula 1 driver, capable of eradicating emotion from the sequence of processes required to win a grand prix, had he also become known as "The Computer." He considered his new "accolade" ridiculous, but it stuck nevertheless, because there was some truth to it.

James "The Shunt" Hunt—later also known as "Superstar," or "Master James"—was the most emotionally charged top-line GP driver since pre–World War II legend Tazio Nuvolari, the wiry,

----

OPPOSITE: Lauda exits the Österreichring's daunting Rindtkurve during his Formula 1 debut at the 1971 Austrian GP. He picked a bad day for it—August 15—because even March star Ronnie Peterson was uncompetitive at this sweeping track. Engine problems caused Lauda to miss a day of practice, and he qualified on the back row. His race was interrupted by an early pit stop for a new tire, and lasted just 20 laps before yet more engine woes curtailed his run. His March 711, converted from Alfa Romeo to Cosworth power for his one-off outing, features the raised front wing conceived by British aerodynamicist Frank Costin. **ABOVE:** Fashion and personal appearance were never high on Hunt's list of priorities. Finding the money to run his Formula Ford was a much more important consideration at the time this photograph was taken.

Lauda and Hunt were cheese and chalk.
And so they were mates. Good ones, who saw beyond their nicknames, and recognized much of themselves in each other.

leathery Italian who would urge his car on as though it were a horse and berate his mechanics at pit stops. But "The Flying Mantuan" never vomited because of nervous tension. Hunt did. Regularly. Usually it overcame him just moments before he wriggled into his car. Often it was done in full view. Occasionally it—mostly dry retching—occurred during a race.

Lauda and Hunt were cheese and chalk.

And so they were mates. Good ones, who saw beyond their nicknames, and recognized much of themselves in each other. Their similarities of attitude and situation were startling.

Both were bright—smarter than the average racing driver—though they flunked out of their expensive schools. (Lauda forged a college diploma for his parents' "benefit.") And both rebelled against their good conservative families' hopes for them. Lauda's father was a captain of industry who owned several paper-processing plants; Hunt's was a stockbroker/accountant who, like many tens of thousands of others, commuted to London from suburban Surrey.

All four of Wallis Hunt's sons, of whom James Simon Wallis was the eldest, were sent to the prestigious Wellington College, a public school founded in Berkshire as a national monument to the famous military duke. Its primary function was to feed Sandhurst, the British Army's nearby officer-training academy. Although James hated regimentation, uniformity, and conformity, he did pay heed to the school's motto: *Virtutis fortuna comes*. Fortune favors the brave.

The day before his 18th birthday, in August 1965, he attended a no-mark Silverstone club meeting and instantly became hooked by motor racing's speed—the sight, the sound, the smell of it. A mooted plan to attend medical school via a crammer college was scotched forthwith, and this self-pronounced future World Champion—he had at least earned an A in confidence, as had Lauda—bought a crashed, stripped-out Mini. After two years of slogging, scrimping, and saving—he even cut down on smoking to help pay for his new addiction—the cherished machine arrived for its first race on, ahem, homemade hand-cut tires, without

---

OPPOSITE: Hunt drops a wheel of his Formula 3 Lotus 59 onto the dirt exiting South Bank Bend at Brands Hatch during a support race at the 1970 British Grand Prix meeting in July. He won his heat from pole position but finished third in the final. He was, however, just a tenth of a second behind the winning Brabham BT28 of Mike "Blocker" Beuttler: 1-liter F3 was ultracompetitive.

ABOVE: Lauda made his Formula 2 debut at the Speed International Trophy at Mallory Park in March 1971. His Bosch Racing Team March 712M retired from both of the event's 40-lap heats, first with fueling trouble, and later because of an engine problem. Hunt dominated the Formula 3 proceedings at the same meeting, comfortably winning from pole position and setting fastest lap—only for his works March 713 to be disqualified because of an air restrictor irregularity.

windscreen or windows, and with a deck chair for a passenger seat. The scrutineers at Snetterton threw it out.

Teenager Andreas Nikolaus (Lauda was 18 months younger than Hunt) also felt compelled to buy a Mini. He had crashed the Cooper S while it still belonged to a friend's father. He then swapped this in a complicated part-ex deal—he was as crafty with his money as Hunt was naive with his—for a competition Cooper S.

Lauda had been fascinated by cars since childhood—unlike Hunt—and his Damascene motorsport moment occurred in rather grander surroundings: at the Nürburgring for the 1966 German GP. Its upshot was the same, though: convinced wannabe racing driver versus unconvinced parents. Hunt's parents sat on their hands and wished away the horrid business. (They knew their stubborn son better than that, of course.) Lauda's parents flat forbade him to race. (Grandfather "Old Lauda" actively queered Niki's patch with a Viennese bank in a bid to scuttle such a frivolous career choice.)

By 1969, however, resilient and self-reliant James and Niki stood on the bottom rung of the single-seater ladder. Hunt, still living at home, was in his second season of Formula Ford. Lauda, alienated from his family and living with girlfriend Mariella Reininghaus, was in Formula Vee. Both had undertaken menial tasks in garages to feed their obsession. (Hunt also worked as a shelf-stacker, a softhearted ice-cream man, a hospital porter, a high-speed delivery boy for a printing firm, and in telemarketing.) Both interspersed occasional wins with hair-raising accidents. In October 1968, Hunt had emerged from the lake at Oulton Park looking like the *Creature from the Black Lagoon*, having somersaulted through an advertising hoarding moments before splashdown. In early 1969, Lauda cartwheeled along the runway at Aspern in his second FVee race. Strike one Russell-Alexis chassis and one Kaimann.

By 1970, both up to their ears in debt yet seemingly without a care and more determined than ever, they had ascended to Formula 3, where the racing was just as fraught, but faster. Lauda reckoned it crazy—and that he fitted its bill. His new car was written off in its first race.

Hunt had impressed during the latter half of 1969 in an old F3 Brabham, and won a prestigious Grovewood Award as a result. It was official: He was a rising young star, one to watch. Using this as a springboard, he arranged with Lotus Components to run a Type 59, coaxing sponsorship from lubricants firm Molyslip. Yet still he camped at circuits, sometimes went hungry and/or hitchhiked, and occasionally siphoned fuel from an unsuspecting donor.

Lauda aligned himself with the nascent McNamara team, which was founded in the Rhineland by an ex–Green Beret who would eventually go AWOL after the sudden death of his rich wife. Its second attempt at an F3 car scored one win that year, in the hands of Gerold Pankl in July.

Lauda had enjoyed his most competitive Formula 2 outing of 1971 at Rouen.
It was a very different story at this demanding road circuit the following year.
Here his March 722 skirts the cobbles of Nouveau Monde hairpin before retiring
with an engine problem, twice—in heat and final.

Hunt, famous then only for **punching a rival live on BBC television**, would emerge from a Spartan flat to lord it in the rowdy pubs and trendy clubs of the King's Road, as though he were a World Champion already.

An already disenchanted Lauda would end his season in a Porsche 908 two-seater sports-racer that he was scared to spin, never mind crash, so much did he owe on it. He had, however, stayed in F3 long enough to warm to that crazy Englishman.

Hunt and Lauda first raced against each other at Magny-Cours in May. They finished fourth and fifth. By August, they were holding a deep—for young racers, at least—conversation about the potential life-shortening side effect of their profession, and the subsequent need to go long on its attendant fun. They knew better than most how hard each was pushing to compensate for inferior equipment—to be noticed. Plus Hunt's attitude had been keened by the two fatal accidents that marred his first international win, at the narrow and fast Rouen road circuit in June.

By 1971, both driving March cars, albeit in different formulas, they were denizens of West London's nightlife. It was an odd couple—the Bohemian (in the lifestyle sense), and the Austro-Bavarian. Blond, blue-eyed Hunt was a bullish six-footer whose round but powerful shoulders had been honed on tennis and squash courts. Lauda was shy and scrawny. It was obvious which of them was the leader—that is, when multiple bike World Champion Mike "Hollywood" Hailwood wasn't leading them willingly astray.

Hunt, famous then only for punching a rival live on BBC television, would emerge from a Spartan flat to lord it in the rowdy pubs and trendy clubs of the King's Road, as though he were a World Champion already. Blessed with charisma, charm, and chutzpah, his relentless pursuit of the opposite sex often led to his having a girl on each arm, which was handy for Lauda. For in the same way that James possessed a serious, analytical side—and would occasionally attend to his tousled locks—so the earnest Niki, based in a rented flat behind Victoria Station, knew how to let down his mousy brown. It's just that he was subtler about it (though that's not saying much).

If there was an edge to their friendship it was because Lauda had moved ahead in the "game," thanks to a £20,000 bank loan and a resultant Formula 2 rent-a-deal. March, though it gave the impression of being as slick as its F1 sponsor STP's product, was skint. It was a team of gamblers. Its first chassis, a 1969 F3 car, wasn't much good. By March of the following year, it had two cars on the front row at the South African GP. By April, it had scored its first GP victory. If you fail, go

up a notch. No wonder it was prepared to take a punt on wild man Hunt and gleefully accept Lauda's *schillings*. Not for a minute did it think it was nurturing two champions.

Hunt remained in F3 where, despite a strong start, his season swiftly became as patchy as Lauda's. Niki was rarely a match for March star Ronnie Peterson, a Swede with car control to burn but who couldn't test for toffee, while James punctuated his year with crashes, the most spectacular of which occurred at Zandvoort. Marshals nervously approaching the upturned wreck fearing the worst were surprised to be met by earthy Anglo-Saxon invective.

Remarkably, matters would get worse before they got better.

March almost ruined them both in 1972, though the lessons learned in adversity would stand them in good stead. Lauda had gone all in with a ballsy £100,000 loan to buy a seat alongside Peterson in the works F1 team. Niki was racing pitted against his own life insurance. The bank didn't wish him dead. Exactly.

ABOVE: Hunt, a victorious Ronnie Peterson, and runner-up Lauda set off on a parade lap after the final round of the 1972 John Player British Formula 2 Championship at Oulton Park in September. Despite driving a year-old March fitted with a smaller-capacity Ford BDA engine, Hunt had taken the fight to his rivals' works versions throughout the 40-lap race. It was this performance that convinced Hesketh Racing to continue.

March and Peterson had prospered on the track in 1971, "Superswede" finishing second to Stewart in the F1 World Championship and winning the European F2 title. There was to be no repeat in '72. Designer Robin Herd's revolutionary F1 car was called 721X. This was one X that did not mark the spot. Whereas Peterson grappled with it, Lauda's clipped English condemned it after a few laps of Jarama in Spain. He was right: It was no bloody good.

One month later, Hunt sounded off at Monaco. He was *still* in F3 and his patience—only his temper was short—was wearing thin because he knew that this was a make-or-break year. When his works March arrived late and unprepared, he flouted a direct order and drove for another team. March knew the things he'd said to be true—its team indeed was a sideline that lacked everything from focus to enthusiasm—but sacked him nevertheless. Burning a short fuse, Hunt tended to shoot from hip and lip, whereas Niki's complaints were more pragmatic and considered. But neither ever shirked a confrontation; they even sparked a few.

Down and apparently out, Hunt's salvation came in strange forms and at a strange place. Lord Thomas Alexander Fermor-Hesketh, a chubby 21-year-old, and Anthony "Bubbles" Horsley, a chubby 28-year-old, viewed their 1972 F3 adventure as a wizard wheeze. They had even commissioned a car from an unproven source to distance themselves from the hoi polloi.

Running at the back, however, the jolliness had started to wear off by May. The car, a Dastle, was tidy but uncompetitive, while Horsley, returning to the cockpit after a long layoff, was both untidy and uncompetitive. Reinforcements were clearly required.

Horsley knew Hunt via a mutual friend. He knew that he was quick and, more importantly, available. His "official" approach was made in an old army tent in the middle of a Belgian field. That is to say, the latrines at the ad hoc Chimay road circuit. Hunt, who had managed to blag one more outing in their mutual friend Chris Marshall's March, was in no position to refuse: McNamara, Dastle, whatever—a drive was a drive.

Theirs was not an instant fix. Hunt crashed at the feet of "The Good Lord," aka "Le Patron," on his debut with the team, and back-to-back accidents for he and Horsley at the British GP meeting in July burst the Dastle bubble.

There remained one last roll of the dice: an old F2 chassis that Hunt's helpers wangled from March by way of his severance. He drove it to fifth place in the Formula Libre Rothmans 50,000

- -

OPPOSITE: Hunt's March 712M heads Lauda's March Engineering 722 at Oulton Park's Old Hall Corner. Hunt led briefly and shared fastest lap with winner Ronnie Peterson, also driving a works March, and Lauda, but eventually finished third. Lauda's second place was sufficient for him to secure the 1972 British Formula 2 title, four points ahead of Peterson.

race at Brands, and then mixed it with the works F2 cars of Peterson and Lauda at Oulton Park in September: He led briefly and set joint-fastest lap before finishing third. Hunt and Hesketh Racing had their egos and mojo back.

Now it was Lauda's turn to salvage something from his wreckage. He, too, had been left high and dry by March, itself on the cusp of bankruptcy. (Lauda briefly considered driving at speed into a brick wall, so great was his debt.) He, too, had a meeting with a "peer"—that living caricature and congenital bluffer, Louis Stanley, known jokingly as "Lord Trumpington." Once the MD of London's Dorchester Hotel, but long of BRM's hierarchy by way of marriage, it was rare for grandiose "Big Lou" to be out-bullshitted, yet not only was he wooed by Lauda's promise of £80,000—money he didn't have, and had no chance of raising—but he also agreed to its payment by installments. Lauda, trusting purely to talent in 1973, had until the deadline for the second payment to prove himself.

Hesketh Racing matched this doubling of the odds: If you fail, go up a notch. Disappointed by the performance and costs of its 1973 Surtees F2 car, it decided that it might as well be "failing" in F1. March was approached, and a (new) chassis purchased. With it came Herd's right-hand man, Dr. Harvey Postlethwaite—"They got me drunk!"—and ace mechanic Nigel Stroud. The team with a silver spoon in its mouth now had a spine of steel.

That season was the making of Hunt and Lauda. The more bhp you slotted behind them, the more pressure you placed them under, the better "Shunt" and "Rat" performed. They were unusual in this respect: F3 normally sorts the wheat from the chaff.

James finished third on his F1 debut—the non-championship Race of Champions at Brands in March—at the wheel of a Surtees TS9B past its best. His March 731, tweaked by "Doc" and screwed together and spannered by "Ball of String," "Ferret," and "Rabbit," was far superior. Though denied points on his World Championship debut in May at Monaco by an engine failure, he finished sixth, fourth, and third at the French, British, and Dutch Grands Prix. He was the apple of his team's eye.

Lauda was envious of his friend's situation at so focused an outfit. BRM, in contrast, was a three-car team that had bitten off more than it could chew. Niki, however, had no choice but

---

OPPOSITE: Lauda and Hunt duel at Copse Corner during their impressive performances in the infamous 1973 British Grand Prix at Silverstone. The Firestone tires on Lauda's BRM P160E are tailing off following a brief spell in second place, and Hunt's March 731 is closing in for the kill. They would finish 12th and 4th respectively. Hunt's car featured the old-style air box. Its new one, designed by Dr. Harvey Postlethwaite, had been damaged during the multicar accident that forced the original race to be restarted after just one lap.

OPPOSITE: Lauda guides the Alpina-run BMW 3.0 CSL he shared with Hans-Joachim Stuck to victory in the Touring category at the 1973 Spa 1000 Km. They finished seventh overall. This race was a World Sportscar Championship encounter, but Lauda also contested selected rounds of the European Touring Car Championship with the team. His wage and winnings—he won the four-hour race at Monza in March alongside Australian Brian "Yogi" Muir—were sufficient to pay the first installment of the money he had promised the Marlboro BRM Formula 1 team.

ABOVE: Hunt and Lauda are joined by debutant Ian Scheckter—elder brother of Jody—for the drivers' briefing at the 1974 South African Grand Prix at Kyalami. Hunt's overalls bear his famous "Sex—Breakfast of Champions" badge. Lauda had registered a first Formula 1 pole position, and his Ferrari 312 B3 would lead the first nine laps before being overtaken by Carlos Reutemann's Brabham. He looked secure in second place, however, until his engine succumbed to fading oil pressure and ignition problems just four laps from home. Hunt, giving Hesketh its World Championship debut as a constructor, retired early because of a broken driveshaft, and Scheckter soldiered to 13th in Team Gunston's Lotus 72E.

to sign when Stanley, now wise to his financial shenanigans, shoved an unappetizing two-year contract under his nose. This was done after Lauda had qualified third at Monaco. Lou was impressed.

So was Enzo Ferrari.

At Silverstone, Lauda and Hunt swerved through the chaos triggered by Jody Scheckter's spinning McLaren. At the restart, Niki's P160E shot from the fourth row to slot briefly into second place. But when its Firestones wilted, so those on Hunt's March blossomed: James set fastest lap and finished just 3.4 seconds behind the winner.

Lauda led for 17 laps in Canada in September, only for Hunt to trump that a fortnight later at Watkins Glen by finishing a harrying second to the season's fastest combination: Peterson in a Lotus 72. Now he had caught Enzo's eye, too. (As had Peter Revson and Jean-Pierre Jarier.) Lord Hesketh swung by Maranello in his private plane, ostensibly to discuss a possible engine deal. He failed to show Enzo sufficient respect, and made it clear that Hunt was not for sale.

But what about that scrawny kid with the funny teeth?

Lauda's technical grasp—particularly on the tire front—and concentration, energy, and speed had impressed his BRM teammate Clay Regazzoni. When "Regga" rejoined Ferrari for 1974, he told *Il Commendatore* that he could do much worse than sign this bright young Austrian. Enzo agreed. Suddenly Lauda was a Ferrari driver—pending court case with BRM notwithstanding. More pressure. Excellent.

Its timing was propitious. Ferrari, deep in a slump, was restructuring. New team manager Luca Cordero di Montezemolo, another bright young thing, was about to instill much-needed calm, common sense, and communication. Mercurial design genius Mauro Forghieri was back in favor and brimming with ideas. The long-distance sports-car program, once deemed Ferrari's most important, had been canned. And the Fiorano test track across the road from the factory had bedded in. Upon his first visit Niki wondered aloud why Ferrari didn't win every GP.

The 1974 season was all about succeeding the retired Stewart as F1's benchmark. Nobody quite managed it, though McLaren's new recruit Emerson Fittipaldi won the drivers' title. McLaren also won the constructors' championship. These were its first world honors.

Lauda opened his F1 account with two wins. Hunt won once.

OPPOSITE: Hunt prepares to board his Hesketh 308 prior to the 1975 Dutch Grand Prix at Zandvoort. The race started in wet conditions—hence the deeply treaded tires—but it was a brave early decision to switch to slicks that gave Hunt his advantage in the race. He had tossed away leads in the past, but not this time; his breakthrough win was secured. The Aurora branding on his overalls and crash helmet referred to a thrusting rival to Scalextric. Hunt was becoming increasingly marketable—even if his patrician team shunned such base overtures.

Lauda graduated first—**and with World Championship honors**—when nine more poles this time resulted in five victories in 1975.

Hunt's victory was scored in Lauda's absence at Silverstone's non-championship International Trophy. With a mesmeric performance, he charged through the order after a sticking clutch and sheared gear knob plunged him down the field having qualified on pole position. But, at 60 percent of a GP distance, this race was indicative of the preparedness of Hesketh as a fledgling constructor. Postlethwaite's neat 308 design was on the pace immediately, but found reliability harder to come by: Witness Hunt's three podium appearances from five GP finishes.

Ferrari, too, was far from perfect: Two wins were poor reward for Lauda's nine pole positions.

Neither driver, however, was free from error. Hunt, in the March, spun away a brief lead at the opening round in Argentina, and Lauda's title hopes ended in Mosport's barriers in late September. There were extenuating factors on each occasion—an absent clutch and unflagged scattered stones over a blind brow—but both men knew they were not yet the finished article.

Lauda graduated first—and with World Championship honors—when nine more poles this time resulted in five victories in 1975. Forghieri's fantastic 312 T, completed by its exquisite transverse gearbox, had been the final cog in the machine.

Hesketh's reliability struggle continued—and Hunt again spun away the lead in Argentina—but then everything clicked at Zandvoort in June. Third-place James pitted boldly early—a familiar strategy today that he pretty much invented—for slicks on a drying track, and, having already plumped for suitable stiffer suspension settings, assumed the lead when the rest followed his example. Lauda harried him for the last 35 laps, but this time no mistake was forthcoming from "The Shunt."

Although Niki had his eyes on a greater, more distant prize that day, he was keenly aware that Hunt's genie might have just escaped its bottle.

It had. Rats!

Magic was about to happen.

- -

OPPOSITE: Ferrari teammates Lauda and Clay Regazzoni—second and third on the day—seem pleased for Hunt after the 1975 Dutch Grand Prix. Their Ferrari 312 Ts, having comfortably stitched up the front row at Zandvoort, had been expected to dominate, but Hunt and Hesketh Racing outsmarted them in changeable conditions.

CHAPTER 2

No Catching Niki

Winning grands prix is a knack.

Lauda, the derided driver who had tried to buy success in Formula 1, was suddenly bang on the money for the world's most famous team, making it look easy and getting paid well for doing so. A smooth operator had emerged from his rough ride through the lower formulas. Now they called him "Super Rat" or "King Rat."

He ended his championship-winning 1975 with a controlled flag-to-flag victory from pole position at Watkins Glen in America, and in January he picked up where he had left off by winning in Brazil. Then he won in South Africa—and in Belgium and Monaco (both from pole), and (for a time) in Spain.

OPPOSITE: Respected Austrian journalist Helmut Zwickl questions an under-the-weather Lauda at Paul Ricard. Ferrari had been on the pace in France, but at the same time showed a chink in its armor when both cars retired because of engine failure. Lauda thus sensed a swing in momentum even before Hunt was re-awarded his Spanish Grand Prix victory by the governing body the following Monday. This would be reflected in the book that Zwickl was writing about Lauda's season. **ABOVE:** Hunt gives team boss Teddy Mayer the lowdown on his M23's newfound handling problems while seated on Zolder's flimsy-looking pit wall. Hunt's robust defensive driving during the Belgian Grand Prix earned him few friends before his gearbox gave up the ghost on lap 36. He was in fifth place at the time, but his engine would have failed in any case.

In a skewed bid to bring order to his life—and perhaps envious of Lauda's long-term and robust relationship with levelheaded brewing heiress, Mariella Reininghaus—**he had married Suzy Miller, a willowy blonde model** (of course).

When he didn't win he finished on the podium (at Long Beach and in Sweden). Strictly business, no fuss—despite a softening left-rear tire in South Africa, and two still-knitting broken ribs in Spain and Belgium.

His knack had become a habit. And nothing was allowed to interfere with it. He even got married in secret.

Hunt, meanwhile, was embroiled in the world's most public divorce. In a skewed bid to bring order to his life—and perhaps envious of Lauda's long-term and robust relationship with levelheaded brewing heiress, Mariella Reininghaus—he had married Suzy Miller, a willowy blonde model (of course) in October 1974. He had regretted the idea from the moment of its proposal, and walked down the aisle of West London's baroque Brompton Oratory full of drink and doubt. He was soon looking for a way out, and was delighted when another man won his wife's heart.

For a woman supposedly yearning for a quiet life, Suzy didn't half pick 'em. Her new beau was the "Mark Antony" to Liz Taylor's "Cleopatra" in the 20th century's most famous love affair: Welsh thespian and serial romancer Richard Burton. They met during Christmas 1975 while skiing at Gstaad (of course), and the press was over it in a flashbulb. Hunt matched Burton in the acting stakes until the divorces were finalized in Haiti (of course), in June.

(The irony is that Lauda had split from Mariella and married Marlene Knaus, whom he'd whisked away from actor Curd Jürgens, the German-speaking "Burton.")

In a weird way—he was a strange guy in lots of ways—James felt he had done his duty by Suzy, and so now was able to roam the sexual field with a clear conscience: a South African actress and a (female) ex-Portuguese army officer here, a British actress and a Swedish model there. And, from Wednesdays to Sunday afternoons on grand prix weekends, he felt better able

---

OPPOSITE: He smoked and he drank, and some of his "training" was conducted in a horizontal position in the company of others, but Hunt was naturally fit and tremendously strong. He held an edge—for now—over Lauda in this respect. He reveals his physique at Paul Ricard.

to concentrate on his motor racing. Fate had awarded him fantastic opportunity, and he was determined to take it.

McLaren and its sponsor Marlboro had been caught on the hop by Emerson Fittipaldi's decision to join his elder brother Wilson's team for 1976—a step down in competitiveness, sweetened by a huge wage from Brazil's giant Copersucar concern. So it was at the tail end of November when McLaren's momentarily disoriented team boss Edward Everett Mayer—called "Teddy" to his face, and "The Wiener" behind his back—rang Hunt.

Lord Hesketh's wallet and will had run dry one week previously, and James, loyal to a fault in this regard, found himself stranded, having turned down Lotus—from whom he didn't receive so much as a free lunch, never mind a promise of a decent wage. But then Emerson's manager rang to give him the heads-up and two hours' grace to compose himself before the inevitable call from McLaren: James wasn't just fast, he was the only available, "suitable" candidate. It was Dastle multiplied by 100.

Neither side knew what to expect of a deal finalized within 36 hours of touching base. Mayer was not alone among the paddock establishment in viewing Hesketh's hellfire antics with

bemusement. His McLaren was in the business of winning, and treated F1 as a science rather than fun. As for Hunt, he had spent three seasons without a teammate to measure himself against. Would this barely rounded peg fit in such a square hole?

True to form, Hunt went at it hammer and tongue (*sic*).

His M23 chassis still unable to comfortably accommodate his big feet and long legs by the time it arrived in São Paulo for the Brazilian GP, Hunt, now known by the mechanics as the "Hunchback of Colnbrook," bitched like hell and demanded changes—a longer cockpit surround among them—that Mayer countermanded because of their unknown impact on the aerodynamics. (Hold on to that thought!)

- -

OPPOSITE: To the runner-up, the spoils: Hunt collects one of his rewards for finishing second to Lauda at Kyalami. Lauda's margin of victory was just 1.3 seconds. **ABOVE:** A jubilant Scuderia Ferrari greets its conquering hero after his South African Grand Prix victory—achieved despite a deflating left-rear Goodyear over the closing three laps of Kyalami. To the left stands chief mechanic Ermanno Cuoghi. In the background stands Stirling Moss, complete with sideburns. The greatest driver never to become World Champion was waiting to interview Lauda for television.

Stirling Moss (second left) and Jackie Stewart (back to camera) join Hunt and Lauda in the Kyalami pit lane. Ex-racing drivers Moss and Stewart, who were involved in the race's television broadcast, provided an interesting comparison—to and with—the current pacesetters in Formula 1. Raffish Moss gravitated toward Hunt's freewheeling spirit and hard-charging style, whereas the more stoic Stewart preferred Lauda's more calculating approach.

James refused to back down, too, and continued to bawl, this time about suspension settings: he didn't like the heavy steering. Not only did Mayer view such aspects of the sport as being the team's business rather than the driver's, but time was too short for them to be achieved: The mechanics, ears flapping to catch the argument, had been too busy effecting an engine swap as the final hour of practice ticked way.

Twenty minutes remained when Hunt, in a frothing lather, attacked the tightly coiled Interlagos track. There was a smoothness to his driving. Always 100 percent committed, particularly in fast corners, he was not, however, hard on his machine, and although he was not immune to bouts of red mist, the cockpit was his oasis of calm. He knew precisely what he was doing—as he had in the pits. Shouting and swearing was his way of grabbing the team's attention. He wasn't unobtrusive Mr. Fittipaldi; he was (occasionally) abusive Mr. Hunt, a driver used to being the focal point. So deal with it!

McLaren, meanwhile, had unknowingly unleashed his beast within by raising its hackles. (Hesketh had eventually learned to stage-manage delays in order to achieve the same ramping effect on Hunt's qualifying performance.) When James returned with pole position—his first in F1, and McLaren's first since Canada 1974—all was forgiven. But not forgotten.

Mayer, who had been with the team since its 1963 inception, was adamant that a McLaren had never been driven so quickly, while a driver who was fast, fun, and feisty instantly persuaded the mechanics. This was not going to be boring.

Down at un-Latin-like Ferrari, Lauda was familiarizing himself with a slightly narrower rear track on his trusty 312 T, and with a new team manager: ex-Fiat rally man Daniele Audetto. Theirs would be a tetchy relationship, but the problems caused by Luca di Montezemolo's departure, via promotion within Fiat, would not be felt fully for several months yet.

ABOVE: The unusual demands of the constant-radius banked corners of Anderstorp, venue for the Swedish Grand Prix, have left Lauda bemused. His Ferrari understeered and oversteered during practice—unusually, he spun—and he started the race from the third row. Luckily for Lauda, Hunt's McLaren was suffering similar problems—and many more spins. Typically Lauda drove a cagey race and finished third, whereas the feistier Hunt surprised himself by doing likewise, to finish fifth. **OPPOSITE:** Smoking in the pits? Er, Hunt did much worse in his day. This is at Long Beach. The urgency of the drag might suggest to some that this was taken after his early-race clash with Patrick Depailler's Tyrrell rather than before it, but the nervy Hunt also behaved like this during the countdown to a start.

OPPOSITE: Lauda and his new team manager Daniele Audetto perch on the pit wall in downtown, down-at-the-heels Long Beach. The latter, promoted from Fiat's successful World Rally Championship team, proved a disappointment to Lauda, who greatly missed the calm and command that Luca di Montezemolo had brought to this demanding and vital role in the sport's most politicized team, from 1974–75. Audetto, a former co-driver for Montezemolo, would go on to enjoy a varied career that embraced powerboats, superbikes, and Indy cars, as well as Formula 1. ABOVE: A chastened Emerson Fittipaldi is pushed to safety after deranging his nose cone against a barrier during a Friday practice session at Long Beach. He admitted that he had been trying to throw his FD04 around "like a go kart." Although the two-time World Champion's decision to join his brother Wilson's team had raised eyebrows, his season had started promisingly with a third-row grid slot at home in Brazil, tailing away thereafter. He finished sixth here in California to score his first point with the team, but could muster only two more in the remaining races. By common consensus, however, he was driving as well as he ever had. A waste of talent.

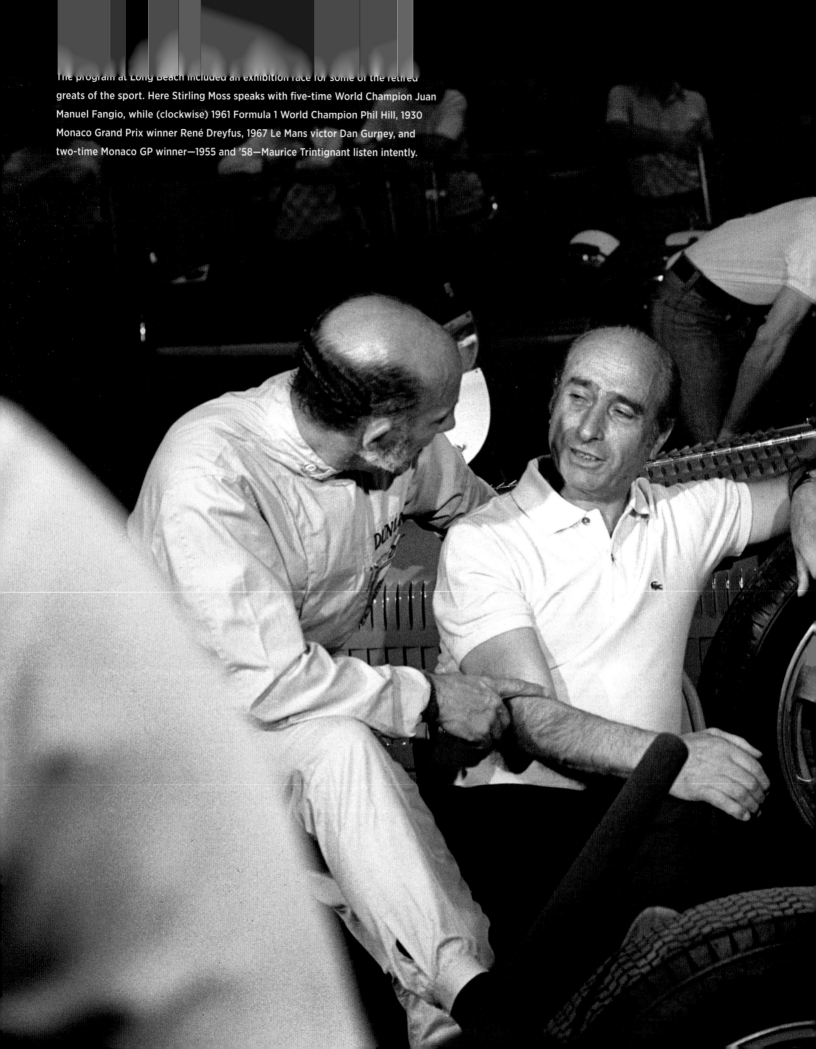

The program at Long Beach included an exhibition race for some of the retired greats of the sport. Here Stirling Moss speaks with five-time World Champion Juan Manuel Fangio, while (clockwise) 1961 Formula 1 World Champion Phil Hill, 1930 Monaco Grand Prix winner René Dreyfus, 1967 Le Mans victor Dan Gurney, and two-time Monaco GP winner—1955 and '58—Maurice Trintignant listen intently.

Blimey, how does he drive this? The gangly Hunt squeezed into Lauda's Ferrari before practice at Zolder's Belgian Grand Prix. Getting out proved tricky, too—much to the amusement of the Scuderia's mechanics. Hunt, with his long legs, big feet, and curved back had had a lot of trouble fitting the McLaren M23, which was a far bigger car than designer Mauro Forghieri's precision-fit 312 T2. That nobody seemed to mind this invasion of privacy was indicative of more-relaxed times within the paddock.

Hunt's pole was no more than a tremor—in any case, Lauda was less surprised by it than most—and the Ferraris controlled the race, Clay Regazzoni leading until slowed by a right-front puncture on the ninth lap.

The second round at Kyalami followed a similar pattern: Hunt made a tentative start from pole—his worry of a burnt clutch was a motif—and Lauda led throughout. This time, however, McLaren's new man followed him closely home in second place. In Brazil, a loose inlet trumpet had jammed the M23's throttle open, the resultant spin into the catch-fencing conclusively damaging its rear-mounted oil coolers. (Hold on to that thought, too!)

By the time of April's United States Grand Prix West—blithely called the "Monaco of the Pacific," despite this LA neighborhood's seedy porn cinemas and run-down, by-the-hour hotels, one of which was gutted by fire during the meeting—Hunt had notched his first victory for McLaren, at the non-championship Race of Champions. His delight, however, was tempered by disappointment at Lauda's retirement at Brands Hatch because of a leaking brake pipe on the new 312 T2. Hunt felt he had the measure of the Ferrari and had been denied the opportunity to prove it. He would have only himself to blame for the same problem in downtown Long Beach.

It was an inspired Regazzoni's turn to dictate—pole position, followed by a start-to-finish romp—but Hunt and McLaren, neither of whom had a history of covering themselves in glory on street circuits, were in the mix. That was until James tangled with the Tyrrell of Patrick Depailler

----

OPPOSITE: Complexity revealed: Six wheels mean more of everything. The Belgian Grand Prix was the first occasion that Tyrrell ran two of its Derek Gardner–designed Project 34 cars. Patrick Depailler was already a convert, but colleague Jody Scheckter had yet to be convinced; he never would be entirely. The idea behind the twinned sets of small wheels was to reduce frontal lift while increasing the contact patch of the tires and the swept area of the brakes. For this outing the Tyrrells were fitted with a much smaller air box, but even this would be shed in later races to improve the airflow over the rear wing. At Zolder, Depailler retired because of an engine failure when holding fourth place—a position that his teammate inherited and held to the finish. Not bad for a nonbeliever. Ultimately this radical design would lag because of Goodyear's failure to maintain the development of its 10-inch diameter rubber—but not before it had won a grand prix. Other teams would build a six-wheeled Formula 1 car, but neither the March 2-4-0 nor the Williams FW08B ever raced. FOLLOWING PAGES: McLaren's think tank (from left)—Teddy Mayer, Hunt, Jochen Mass, and the M23's designer, Gordon Coppuck—attempt to extricate themselves from the morass they find themselves in at Monte Carlo. Both cars ran five-speed gearboxes rather than their usual six-, and Mass's car featured a front wing mounted at gearbox level at the rear—but there were to be no quick fixes. Hunt retired, and Mass did well to finish fifth in a car that was fundamentally too bulky for the tight confines of this track. McLaren in its original guise of Bruce McLaren Motor Racing had made its grand prix debut at this circuit 10 years before, but the team would not win Formula 1's most prestigious race until 1984. Since then, however, it has prevailed there a record 15 times.

Lauda finished second at Long Beach. He was still on top of his job, until **his world would flip upside down a few weeks later** when the tractor he was driving at his Austrian home overbalanced.

on lap four, the Frenchman oblivious to his rival's lunge because he was untangling a moment of his own while holding second place. A puce Hunt stood on the track, just off the racing line and around a blind bend, for several laps to vent his spleen before stalking off to continue his haranguing of Depailler—F1's "Little Boy Lost"—at the post-race press conference. As he did so, a McLaren mechanic restarted his relatively undamaged car and trundled it back to the pits.

It had not been Hunt's finest hour. He later admitted that his had been a rash move against a driver he listed as "unreliable"—he kept a mental file on all his opponents—yet he remained unrepentant for his actions and outburst. Perhaps the split from Suzy had upset him more than he had let on.

His public antics and "private" life meant the whole world was suddenly aware of him, and F1. Little wonder that 75,000 people turned up to witness his next escapade: the non-championship International Trophy at Silverstone. There, he proved to be in a class of his own in Lauda's absence: relaxed, fast, and undramatic. Perhaps the first glimpse of the James so feared by Niki.

Lauda, coping calmly with flat-spotted front tires and latterly with a worrying whine from the transmission—finished second at Long Beach. He was still on top of his job, until his world would flip upside down a few weeks later when the tractor he was driving at his Austrian home overbalanced. His injuries were considered a lucky escape.

All seemed well—from the outside, at least—three weeks later at Zolder for the Belgian GP. Lauda, who was still receiving pain-numbing injections, wasn't happy with the balance of his car, even though he started from pole position and led throughout. The concern was that this race marked the start of the season's grind—a race every other weekend, the bulk of them in unglamorous Northern Europe—and so spare time was short, making any underlying problems harder to put right. Lauda's subsequent win in Monaco—the most dominant of his five from

---

OPPOSITE: Having started from pole position for a third consecutive year in this Mediterranean principality, Lauda led every lap of the Monaco Grand Prix to score his second straight victory at the venue. (He had led all bar one lap in 1975.) With five wins and a second place from the six rounds to date, he was 36 points ahead of his nearest rival. It was only May, and yet a second consecutive world title seemed in the bag. Here his Ferrari 312 T2 leads the lapped Lotus 77 of Gunnar Nilsson, who is soon to retire because of an engine failure.

the six races so far—convinced Ferrari's command chain that little, if anything, was broken and needed to be fixed. That was an understandable but dangerous assumption.

McLaren was at the opposite end of the spectrum, tearing out its hair—with which it was luxuriantly appointed—at its inability to fix a car that had, according to Hunt, suddenly "turned evil." Oversteering everywhere, James drove his unruliest race of the season at Zolder before his gearbox seized (the engine would have blown in any case, apparently). At Monaco, he qualified 14th, removed his engine's air box in a bid to regather some rear downforce, and retired with a blown engine, having already spun to the back of the snake in his frustration. At Anderstorp in Sweden, he spun and spun and spun again in practice, qualified eighth—and rated his patient drive to fifth as one of his best. The two points it garnered would certainly prove very important.

Lauda also struggled in Sweden. He talked of a tired flat-12 after qualifying, and of cold Goodyears and the resultant understeer/oversteer after finishing third. Hardly disastrous given his championship lead of 32 points, but a worrying indicator nevertheless.

The sea change blew in under a Mediterranean July sky at Paul Ricard. Lauda arrived suffering from a summer cold; Hunt arrived with a car fully recovered and promptly secured his fourth pole of the season. A decision to start on soft tires with 50 laps beneath them and therefore "cured" in a bid to secure more consistency during a hot, dry race meant that the increasingly savvy Hunt was not too concerned when Lauda, on lightly scrubbed rubber, bolted into the lead. Plus James could see an ominous vapor curling from the Ferrari's tail.

Lauda's engine let go on lap 9, and teammate Regazzoni's blew up on lap 19 while he was keeping leader Hunt honest. Now this was deeply serious. Ferrari prided itself above all else on the reliability of its engine, which was holding an edge over the majority's V8 Cosworth-DFV in terms of bhp and, more importantly, torque. The immediate problem was traced to tiny cracks in a crankshaft flange. The Scuderia's deeper-rooted malaise exhibited cracks that were larger and metaphorical. They could not be fixed in its foundry. Or in a hurry.

This was no time to panic—after all, Lauda was renowned as the arch methodical tester—but the fact that Hunt had won two grands prix in two days was a powerful wake-up call.

- -

OPPOSITE: Formula 1 cars of the period had a "dragster" look because of their huge rear tires and small fronts. Traction had been the buzzword since the arrival of wings in the late 1960s, and designers had tended to shift weight rearward to facilitate this. Ferrari's 312 Ts, however, marked a change in thinking. Designer Mauro Forghieri centralized their mass by moving the driver forward within its wheelbase and fitting a shorter transverse gearbox. This improved the car's ability to change direction and made better use of increasing levels—and understanding—of downforce by spreading it more equally between front and back. That said, the 312 T2 used 20-inch-wide rear Goodyears in 1976. While his mechanics sort through his sets in readiness for the Swedish Grand Prix, Lauda catches a few moments with wife Marlène on the Anderstorp pit wall.

CHAPTER 3

Jarama Brouhaha

How so, two wins in two days?

Well, one on the track, then one in the courtroom.

The Spanish Grand Prix at the aptly twisty Jarama on the outskirts of Madrid was always going to be a political bunfight. The Formula 1 Constructors' Association—with its acronym at that time, F1CA—had invited the Commission Sportive Internationale (CSI), the sporting arm of the Fédération Internationale de l'Automobile (FIA), to get a grip on category, fervent in the hope that it would make a hash of it.

OPPOSITE: Measured: Hunt stays off the curbs. His M23 featured a new twin-eared air box to comply with the changed regulations. A front roll hoop, visible behind the windscreen and ahead of the steering wheel, had been fitted so that a theoretical line connecting its uppermost point to the peak of the rear roll hoop allowed 5 centimeters' clearance above the driver's crash helmet. McLaren brought three cars to Jarama. Two were in updated spec and one remained in the old; that's because the new rules did not apply until May 1, and Friday practice fell on April 30. Call it attention to detail.

ABOVE: Hunt and Gunnar Nilsson celebrate their first and third places as King Juan Carlos looks on. This was the Swedish Lotus driver's third grand prix appearance. His result was achieved despite an increasingly heavy gear change and a Cosworth DFV that refused to pull maximum revs.

It did.

CSI had the year before lost its race-date and sanctioning powers. Now its rulebook was in question. In a bid for clarification, a host of new maximum dimensions were to be applied to the cars and adhered to as from this race. The most obvious change was the lopping of the tall air boxes. The friction that lit the fire, however, was measured in fractions.

The big news initially was the emergence from a woodshed in Surrey of the six-wheeled Tyrrell P34. Patrick Depailler qualified his 4-2-0 on the second row and was running in fourth place when it suffered brake failure after 25 laps.

Attention then turned to the increasingly familiar battle at the front between Lauda and Hunt. Injured Niki was toughing it out in the lead, and James was mercilessly biding his time. The latter reckoned his move, which came on lap 32 (of 75), was of the type possible only against a racer that you respected and trusted. Niki said his swerve in avoidance felt "like a knife." A popped rib almost punctured a lung, and there could be no retaliation from him that day. Their rivalry was hotting up.

As was that between Hunt and teammate Jochen Mass, the man who replaced him as a works March F3 driver back in 1972. The Bavarian, the elder by almost a year, had been with McLaren since the last two races of 1974, quietly learning his craft and earning the team's respect. Having scored his maiden GP victory in Spain in 1975—albeit in very different circumstances to those at Jarama (the race on Barcelona's Montjüich Park road circuit was halted when a car crashed into the crowd)—he saw no reason to accede to Hunt's assumed primacy.

Indeed, he had scored more points—seven plays six—than him over the first three races. Though Jochen smiled whenever Hunt called him "Herman the German," he was riled by it. And joshing James was smart enough to know that. Mass in turn knew that steady sixth and fifth places were insufficient when faced by such a force of nature. So he drew up to Hunt's gearbox to make his point, set the fastest lap on lap 52—and suffered an engine failure on lap 65. Hunt would later complain to the team about Jochen's monstering tactics. He would never have to worry about them again. Mass, almost a busted flush, was shunted further down McLaren's list of priorities by what happened next.

Half an hour after taking the checkered flag, the winning M23 was declared illegal and disqualified. It was 1.8 centimeters too wide. That Gordon Coppuck's three-year-old design, the longest and widest in the entry, had been used as the template for the new regulations

----

OPPOSITE: Hunt at the office. Note the as-yet-unpainted metal spacer next to his right shoulder inserted to allow him extra room in the cockpit.

Hunt greets the checkered flag ahead of Clay Regazzoni. The latter endured a disappointing race: He qualified fifth, and was holding that position during the race when his fuel pressure gauge sprang a leak and sprayed his legs with fuel. His mechanics stemmed the flow as best they could, but the necessary pit stop cost "Regga" three laps, and he trailed home in 11th place.

Injured Niki was toughing it out in the lead, and James was mercilessly biding his time. The latter reckoned his move, which came on lap 32 (of 75), was of the type **possible only against a racer that you respected and trusted.**

only added to the embarrassment of a team that prided itself on attention to detail and got up others' noses because of it. FOCA was an uneasy coalition: The need to win always twanged at its web of alliances.

Teddy Mayer, a smart and scrappy lawyer from Pennsylvania in a previous life, went on a charm offensive. He argued that the transgression was caused by tire-bulge—the Goodyears were still warm when measured after the race—and that there was no performance to be gained from it. Therefore, blame the team rather than punish an unknowing driver by taking away his points, too.

The disqualification of team and driver was confirmed as night drew in.

Mayer appealed to Spain's governing body. Lost. And appealed again, this time to the FIA. The hearing was set for Monday, July 5.

A lot was to happen before then.

Lauda, stiff and sore and pale, was long gone from Jarama by the time his "victory" was confirmed. His T2, distinctive with its new air ducting either side of the cockpit, and 20 pounds lighter and 2.2 inches longer in the wheelbase than its predecessor, had run strongly on its debut, which was just as well, because his anticipated main rival was coming on stronger, too.

Whereas Lauda had helped damp the wilder fires at Ferrari, so Hunt was providing a vital spark at McLaren. Founder Bruce McLaren's calming influence could still be felt six years after his death in a testing accident at Goodwood—and the team remained shot through with a skein of skilled, chilled Kiwi mechanics. The lack of a charismatic leader, however, had been starting to tell, and Hunt was a much-needed shot in the arm. The result was that Ferrari was no longer the most exciting team in the paddock: McLaren was on the front and the back pages, in the glossies and on television and radio, thanks to the eccentricities and caprices as well as skill of its new lead driver.

Easygoing Bruce would have been taken aback by Hunt's "methods," but also would have enjoyed their result. A pet project at the time of his death had been the dramatic M6GT road car aimed squarely at upstaging Enzo's products; becoming a brand was a long-term aim of his.

- -

OPPOSITE: Hunt seems to be having a premonition of the controversy to come. King Juan Carlos, inaugurated the previous November after the death of Spanish dictator General Franco, leads the applause.

OPPOSITE: Patrick Depailler leans on the increased contact patch provided by the six-wheeled Tyrrell P34. The Frenchman, always a bigger fan of this radical design than teammate Jody Scheckter, was selected to give the car its debut. He qualified third—more than a second faster than Jody, in the conventional 007 model—and was holding third place when he ran out of brakes (and road) after 25 laps. The car raced without its original bulky air box in order to improve the airflow around the rear wing. **ABOVE:** Don't make me laugh! Clearly Lauda's painkillers were working here, but his broken ribs hampered him badly during the race.

Hunt's insistence that McLaren and Marlboro accept him as he was rather than attempt to repackage him as a corporate entity was image gold. (There was a blazing row about the wearing of blazers before he put pen to contractual paper.) His pizzazz atop McLaren's (usual) assurance was a potent and exciting combination. It is something that McLaren, still endeavoring to become that global brand, has rarely enjoyed since (during Senna versus Prost, for sure, and perhaps with Lewis Hamilton in 2007).

Even self-proclaimed prickly bastard, the not easily impressed Alastair Caldwell, could see the benefits of Hunt. This English-born Kiwi was the power behind McLaren's throne. Square of jaw and steely of stare, his power struggle with Mayer was its undercurrent. Both felt they ran the team, and so they did—in different ways. Caldwell's heart and loyalty lay with Bruce, and because of this he almost left in the 1970 aftermath. He had joined as a cleaner, was promoted to mechanic after just one day, and had been rising through the ranks ever since. Team manager by 1974, he was not averse to countermanding the orders of Mayer who, as far as Caldwell was concerned, was the guy who dealt with the idiots of the press—of which there were by now hundreds, buzzing and hovering.

Caldwell couldn't give two hoots about the problems Hunt caused his bosses, or the fact that James was the nerviest driver he had ever worked with—chain-smoking, helmet on, helmet off, puking, helmet back on—before a race, and capable of violence for a time after it. (The unwary would receive a shock if ever they tried to "earth" wired James.) All Caldwell cared about where Hunt was concerned was his qualifying speed and race pace—both excellent—and his inability to test. James could see the need, and was envious of Niki's ability in this respect, yet couldn't work up the necessary enthusiasm. Whereas Niki would sit in his race car and munch on a plate of sandwiches during a lunch break at a test, James would be hankering for a trip to the pub. He talked the tech talk in an attempt to cover his tracks, but Caldwell reckoned it bullshit. He pushed Hunt as hard as he dared in testing—he didn't want to kill the "Golden Goose"—and drove his mechanics hard. They called him "Guv."

OPPOSITE (TOP): Lauda glances in his mirror to check the progress of you-know-who. The Austrian led for the first 31 laps. Ferrari's response to the banning of tall air boxes was distinctive: It added ducting that ran down both flanks of the cockpit "conning tower" to each bank of cylinders on its flat-12. **OPPOSITE (BOTTOM):** New brackets for the rear anti-rollbar and longer radius rods allowed McLaren to extend the M23's wheelbase by a further 2 inches. This was done to reposition the rear wing in cleaner air without exceeding the 80-centimeter rule in relation to the vertical centerline of the rear wheels. Also note the new siting of the oil radiators, alongside the engine bay rather than under the rear wing.

Caldwell couldn't give two hoots about the problems Hunt caused his bosses, or the fact that **James was the nerviest driver he had ever worked with**—chain-smoking, helmet on, helmet off, puking, helmet back on.

Luckily, the M23 was already an established front-runner, reasonably easy to dial, responsive to set-up changes, a match for all but the Formula 2-based Marches and six-wheeled Tyrrells in a straight line, and competitive on most types of track. It also possessed useful room for development despite its age. Coppuck's decision to integrate the new-for-1973 safety regulations rather than simply bolt them on was still paying dividends—so much so that his ongoing M26 replacement was held back.

McLaren's experiences with its bulkier Indy cars and ultra-successful two-seater Can-Am cars had convinced it that bigger was always better. Ground effect downforce generated by underbody tunnels was still two seasons distant, but the flat-bottomed M23's large floor area briefly put it at the head of this tentative performance seam. Not only did a NACA duct under the driver create a low-pressure area up through its cockpit, but it was at the vanguard of experimentation with plastic side skirts as a means of sealing the air beneath the car from that around it. These were objected to and removed in South Africa, but then allowed again at Long Beach. McLaren had the inquiring mind, whereas Ferrari was resolutely hard to convince on such matters.

Among McLaren's other developments were a six-speed adaptation of Hewland's gearbox—its narrower ratios a bid to keep the peaky V8 on the boil, and to keep pace with Ferrari's smoother flat-12; and an onboard pneumatic starter that obviated the need for a large and therefore heavy battery. Both innovations were inspired and led by Caldwell.

Ferrari differed in so many ways. McLaren tended to test at circuits scheduled to host a grand prix, whereas Ferrari would pound around Fiorano. This was fine, an advantage, even as long as the team didn't become too insular and isolated. Also, Forghieri's design, a triumph of packaging,

OPPOSITE: French team Ligier was impressive in its first season of Formula 1. Despite now being shorn of its huge air box—nicknamed the "teapot," it provided a perfect site for its sponsor's flamenco-dancing logo—the Matra V12-engined JS5 continued to be competitive. Jacques Laffite was in fifth place when his gear linkage came adrift on lap 24, and two laps were lost in the pits. Like Hunt's McLaren, the Ligier, too, was disqualified after the race—its rear wing was too rearward—only to be reinstated by the FIA. Why Ligier bothered to protest when Laffite had finished a lowly and distant 12th was a mystery.

was one of the smaller cars on the grid. This was fine, another possible advantage, as long as that layout suited the prevalent tires.

Way back in May 1975, Coppuck had convinced Goodyear, learning how to deal with a monopoly after Firestone's withdrawal, to makes tires that would work with his M23. Other teams favored them, too, and they began to come on stream by Jarama. They would be the norm by July. Ferrari should have been all over this like a rash; instead, it spent too much time trying to tune a de Dion rear suspension, a techno throwback that it hoped would cure an inherent instability and improve traction. Lauda reckoned it okay, but no better than the standard car. It might have worked had tires of a less-conservative construction been available.

Ferrari was also failing to adopt new methods and materials. Ground effects would remain anathema to it for several seasons to come, plus it was slow to follow the lead of McLaren and others in the increased use of lighter, stronger Kevlar body panels and components. And although a version of the 312 T2 minus the familiar, presumably reassuring, tubular bracing within its folded "monocoque" would be introduced at Paul Ricard in July, this was another crucial area in which Maranello lagged.

Complacency was setting in, and development was beginning to falter. Team manager Audetto, who never received the freedom to perform that had been awarded to Montezemolo, became increasingly fraught and tangled in short-term internal politics. And Lauda alone was not enough to stem this tide.

In contrast, the problem that initially had prevented McLaren from benefiting from Ferrari's wobble was infuriatingly minor.

Mayer had won a different argument in Spain by laboring the semantics of oil containers and oil radiators. This was in response to the latter's repositioning within the sidepod to the right of the engine bay, which contravened one of the new dimensions. Determined not to give Ferrari any ammunition in the fallout from the post-race wrangling, it was decided to have the items returned to their original positions beneath the rear wing, aft of the transmission. Except theirs wasn't quite the original position. The new rules had narrowed and shortened the available space and forced a minimal compromise, and this inch or so would cause miles of pain.

The change was done between practice sessions at Zolder—the team insisted it was because of overheating worries—and suddenly the car was hopeless. The airflow around the wing had been adversely disturbed and a critical balance lost, and not until the coolers were returned to their side mounting would it return. (Mayer would always insist that the important alteration was subtler than that.)

Belgium and Monaco slid by in a blur of oversteer. But in Sweden, Hunt evinced some hard-won cunning. And when the speed suddenly snapped back into place in France, he was the complete driver. He knew Niki's engine would go bang. No need to rush.

Then, on the Monday afternoon, the FIA's International Court of Appeal returned his Spanish GP win.

Hunt had reduced Lauda's lead by 21 points—from 47 to 26—in the space of two days: a good return on a trifling $3,000 fine, amply covered by the restored prize money. A rattled Enzo called the decision "wicked," while a bemused "Rat" reckoned that a car was either legal or it wasn't, and he had a point.

The hype for the British GP went into overdrive.

And the enmity between Ferrari and McLaren remained supercharged for the next 35 years.

- -

OPPOSITE: Penske had tested its new PC4 model but decided to stick with the PC3—and would continue to do so until the Swedish Grand Prix in June. Here, in John Watson's hands, it leads Carlos Pace's Brabham and the Ensign of Chris Amon. "Wattie'" would retire with engine failure, but his chasers finished sixth and fifth respectively.

CHAPTER 4

Battle of Britain

Brands Hatch sits within a natural amphitheater. Its main grandstand looms over the pits, which are tucked deeply behind a protective wall. There was, however, no hiding place when a crowd, cooked by a heat wave's sun, was informed that its "champion" would not be venturing into battle because of a trivial technicality.

These were not the usual attuned race-goers inured to and understanding of the sport's niceties and not-so niceties. They were Hunt followers scenting blood. Their hero had sounded a trumpet voluntary on television only days before. No, really, he had. At the Albert Hall. And passably well, too. Now he was out to catch "The Rat." There was, it seemed, nothing he couldn't do.

The year before, Hunt had been the patriotic hero, his car carrying the red cross of St. George and the blue of Scotland's Saltire on a virginal white background. Now he was a

---

OPPOSITE: Lauda and Hunt raise the cement dust at Paddock Hill Bend on the second lap after the restart. An expectant crowd fills—almost drips from—every vantage point. The overtaking move they were craning forward to see arrived 43 laps later, down the hill, through the dip, and up the other side of the valley, at Druids hairpin.
ABOVE: Shake on it! Hunt and Lauda's relationship was strong enough to survive the partisan atmosphere. Just. The Duke of Kent looks on, while third-placed (for now) Jody Scheckter takes a reviving swig behind Lauda's right shoulder.

smoking, drinking, toking, shagging motor-racing rock star who crossed social divides thanks to his posh accent and penchant for classical music, his smart mouth and scruffy dress sense: jeans, T-shirt, bare feet. He appealed to girls, guys, gents, and grannies. He was eligible hunk meets unacceptable punk. He was Tesco's in Monaco. He was a lowbrow high roller. He epitomized both the British upper-middle-class ideal of achieving success without apparent effort and the leery, beery lads' perfect night out. Everybody had an opinion about him because nobody could tie him down. Or put a tie on him. Essentially a shy man who relied on a small circle of long-standing trusted friends, the public glare would eventually send him scuttling for the shade of his shell.

For now, however, he basked in it.

He warmed up for his home grand prix with a police chase, a head-on crash into a tree, and a disagreement with Britain's most popular disc jockey, Noel Edmonds, who was co-driving his Vauxhall rally car on the Tour of Britain. This event was a fluffy piece of promotional fun, and Hunt certainly had a laugh—but didn't shed a tear when it came to its sudden early halt.

He would feel differently when the Ferraris of Clay Regazzoni and Lauda tangled at the crest of Paddock Hill Bend.

Lauda had arrived in Britain feeling fit and fresh, and was looking forward to driving a car with the new type of tub. Exuding confidence, he reveled in his appointed role of baddie. He was not a man to be out-psyched. That Luca di Montezemolo was also present for the first time this year suggested that not everybody at Ferrari was so confident or reassured. Trouble was expected.

Lauda mischievously stirred the pot by parking 20 minutes before the end of qualifying and yet still pipping Hunt to pole position by six-hundredths of a second. Britain's hero appeared insouciant as he spoke of scrambling traffic.

Given a choice, Lauda selected to start from the left rank of the grid, on the outside of the track, therefore, but at the top of its slope, and also on the rubbered-in racing line. The crowd of 77,000 willed Hunt to make the most of his inside run, but Regazzoni from the second row was by him in a trice. Macho man Clay, who was listed in James's mental file as "untrustworthy in the early laps," then lunged at Lauda.

Hunt's wry smile upon the Italian cars' collision lasted only until he was punted up the rear and plunged into the melee. His right-rear Goodyear rode over half-spun Regazzoni's corresponding wheel and the McLaren took off. Its arcing flight was graceful; its landing wasn't. The front-left suspension rocker and steering arm were badly bent upon touchdown.

Lauda's Ferrari—its suspension at full bump and maximum roll—tackles the adversely cambered bend that had been recently renamed in the memory of two-time Formula 1 World Champion, Indy 500, and Le Mans 24 Hours winner, Graham Hill.

OPPOSITE: A packed South Bank, basking in the sunshine and Hunt's reflected glory, shows its appreciation. It's unlikely that Lauda is just out of shot! ABOVE: Chief mechanic Ermanno Cuoghi confers with Lauda (bottom left), while a fellow Ferrari team member keeps a wary eye on the crowd. The reformed grid, like the grandstands, was packed and seething with activity.

Hunt saw red (and yellow). Flags, that is. The race was stopped and, accessing his microscopic knowledge of an intimate track that had played a pivotal role in his career, he pulled up at the rear entrance to the paddock rather than force his crippled car on for another whole lap.

The arguments that these events ignited were still raging 50 minutes later. Was the race to be aborted and started afresh, or simply restarted? The 1975 British GP at Silverstone had been halted because of rain, and its result taken from the order of the previous lap. Thus, four cars buried in the fences scored points. Using that as a precedent, the 1976 British GP had yet to officially start.

There were other confusions. Could a driver nominate a team's spare car if his original was beyond repair? Was Hunt still rolling when the red flags fluttered? Must you have completed an entire red-flagged lap to be allowed to restart in your repaired race chassis?

McLaren plonked its spare on the front row, just in case, while Teddy Mayer and Alastair Caldwell—the law and its strong arm—fueled the debate so that their mechanics had sufficient time to fix Hunt's damaged car, just in case.

Ferrari's Daniele Audetto, fitted shirt unbuttoned to the navel and sporting a large pair of sunglasses and a chunky wristwatch—hardly items to endear him to this crowd—was all Latin gestures. Hunt was loud and animated, too—but in an "acceptable" British fashion. Lauda, who had held a big lead at the end of that opening lap, sat tight.

The increasingly restless crowd went ballistic when Hunt's enforced retirement was confirmed because spare cars were not to be allowed. Police feared a riot. The insurgency never got beyond chanting and slow hand-clapping, with the occasional cup and can lobbed onto the track, but it might have done had it not been for the pragmatic decision to start the race with a full complement, with a view to sorting out the mess later.

At which point McLaren reversed its mended car onto the grid. (Both Regazzoni and Ligier's Jacques Laffite would be disqualified while the GP was in progress because they had started in their spare cars.) The British "fighter pilot" would get his shot at his Germanic rival in the red car. Hunt versus the Hun under a Kentish blue sky. It was that fundamental.

The second start was calmer, and the race quickly settled into the battle everyone had come to see: Lauda leading, Hunt on his tail. The McLaren was understeering through left-handers because of the stagger dialed into its chassis by the fitting of tires of different diameters down each side, better to make it handle through the more numerous right-handers. As its fuel load reduced, Hunt was able to "chuck" his car into the lefts to initiate a compensating oversteer. The gap began to shrink.

On lap 45 (of 76), the roles were reversed when Hunt, his "eyes closed," outbraked Lauda into Druids hairpin. The crowd's instantaneous conversion of emotion from pent to spent was so loud that Hunt said he'd heard it above his engine's note. No one disbelieved him.

Once again there would be no fight-back from Lauda—much to Hunt's disappointment. He was bursting to give his hotheaded fans more to shout about, whereas Niki was cool about finishing second. The pair smiled, joked, and shook hands on the podium, but when Lauda explained that gear-selection misgivings had hampered him for much of the race, Hunt sniped that this could only have been after he had passed him. (Both men had been running at almost qualifying speed when Niki set the fastest race lap on 41.)

- -

OPPOSITE: Event Three. Laps completed: 0. Laps to go: 76. Lauda makes good his escape while teammate Clay Regazzoni pays the price for his rashness, steam rising from a damaged radiator. Hunt, hidden behind the askew Ferrari, is about to be launched skyward, while Mario Andretti (5) and Chris Amon (22) take avoiding action. Both Andretti's Lotus and Amon's Ensign suffered early engine failures in the restarted race as a result of problems—wet spark plugs and a loose water-hose clamp—caused by this incident.

The right result on the day—the first Englishman to win the British Grand Prix for 18 years. The restless crowd would go home happy, by which time the political machinations that would eventually rescind this Hunt "victory" were already well under way. Dig those flares! And note that underwhelming single row of Armco.

Given the highly charged atmosphere surrounding it, their relationship was as healthy as could be expected.

McLaren and Ferrari, meanwhile, were at daggers drawn: protests at 20 paces. The Tyrrell and Copersucar teams withdrew their official post-race complaints upon hearing witness statements confirming that Hunt was on the move when the race was halted. Ferrari, however, pressed on with its complaint. Audetto said that he was just doing his job—doing what he was told, in other words.

The FIA Court of Appeal's hearing was scheduled for September 24.

Hunt didn't care. Whatever the eventual outcome, he had beaten Lauda fair and square in terms of outright performance. His championship position meant that the only approach open to him was to go flat out, round by round, which perfectly suited his mood and MO. He was more of an out-and-out racer than was Lauda, and thrived on confidence.

Mayer and Caldwell knew that fell well. In the aftermath of Brands, the former stated that Hunt was the most talented driver McLaren had ever had. The latter suggested that Britain had another

ABOVE: A champagne moment that would ultimately lose its fizz. OPPOSITE: Ferrari mechanics work on Lauda's car in the new, improved (i.e., much wider) pit lane. It's not always noticeable in photographs, but the 312 T2's full-width, one-piece front wing was slightly raised and attached underneath by a pair of adjustable brackets.

If the cap fits. Hunt shows his appreciation of his tire supplier. Goodyear had a monopoly, but increasingly its wares were becoming better suited to the long-wheelbase, wide-track McLaren rather than the smaller Ferrari. Lauda left Brands Hatch sure in the knowledge that the Scuderia had been overtaken in the development race.

Hunt and McLaren were still in their honeymoon period. The man who had pronounced **"sex to be the breakfast of champions"** was happy to be in bed with so racy a team.

Jim Clark on its hands. Hunt, like Lauda, had no racing heroes, but he thought enough of Clark to realize that Caldwell's fulsomeness was a stretch. He appreciated both men's words nevertheless. They neither did harm nor did they ring hollow, for Hunt was improving all the time, being clearly capable now of absorbing pressure as well as applying it.

Lauda, too, knew that Hunt was a match in terms of speed, and could see the balance of power swinging in McLaren's direction despite his regrouping effort in Britain. He wasn't unduly worried, but felt that this was the time to act: He asked Enzo for a new contract. The Old Man's response to this preemptive strike was volcanic; he preferred to leave monetary affairs until much later in a season in order to keep a driver on his toes.

And then Lauda named his price. It sent Enzo's anger off the scale. They had crossed swords and words after the tractor incident—but not like this. Lauda, who was perfectly prepared to walk away, refused to budge or budget, and they traded insults via a translator—an understandably edgy Piero Lardi, yet to be officially recognized as Enzo's illegitimate son. Ferrari called Lauda a "Jew-boy." Lauda reduced his demand fractionally, and a deal was grudgingly agreed upon.

The mood lightened instantly. Lauda could see that his boss had enjoyed their battle—Enzo loved the chase of negotiation more than the kill of the deal itself—and that their mutual respect was still intact. Its shock waves, however, surely unsettled the team. Had Lauda's card been stamped? To whom should I pin my allegiance? Its focus continued to blur.

While Lauda and Ferrari skirted around divorce, Hunt and McLaren were still in their honeymoon period. The man who had pronounced "sex to be the breakfast of champions" was happy to be in bed with so racy a team; the team in turn was delighted with its bargain £45,000 catch. Spirits were high.

Ferrari's could only appear low and cynical opposite such enthusiasm. It won its appeal—and Lauda pronounced himself delighted by the FIA's ruling. If he had any sympathy for McLaren's argument that Ferrari had benefited from a problem its drivers had caused in the first place, he didn't admit it.

Sympathy, either offered or received, had never won any votes with Lauda. He dealt with life's challenges—and near-death experiences—in matter-of-fact absolutes.

CHAPTER 5

Fire in the Forest

Lauda had as little time for superstition and omens as he had for sympathy. In 1973, while holding an impressive fifth place on the second lap of the German Grand Prix, his BRM gave an unnerving twitch before spearing off the road and bouncing for 300 yards along the top of an earth bank. Niki broke his wrist. In 1975, having led the German GP from the start, his Ferrari wobbled unnervingly on lap 9 (of 14), its front-left tire punctured. The resultant pit stop dropped him to fifth, but eventually he recovered to finish third. These incidents were separated by a few hundred yards on a 14-mile circuit.

In the German GP of the intervening year, Lauda "goofed" in his haste to make up for a tardy start from pole position, and he spun into retirement after not much more than a mile.

He insisted that none of the above had any bearing on his public condemnation of the Nürburgring's iconic, mythic, lunatic Nordschleife. He was not in awe of its challenge; he was

- -

OPPOSITE: Now on slicks, Lauda had re-passed Guy Edwards (shown), Brett Lunger, and Harald Ertl by the time they reached Adenau Bridge, 8 kilometers in. The crash, fire, and rescue that would link them together forever are just seconds away. **ABOVE:** Opinionated Lauda makes his point. Not everybody wanted to hear what he had to say on the topic of the Nordschleife, but he was to be proved right in dramatic—almost fatal—fashion.

Lauda spoke from rare experience when he called it **"the ultimate madness."** In his opinion, if you weren't frightened here, you weren't going fast enough.

inspired by it. His 6:58.6 pole time of 1975 made him the first—and forever to remain the only—man to break the seven-minute barrier. He had come closer than most to completing the perfect lap—close enough to realize how crazy he had been to attempt such a feat, as had multiple World Champion Juan Manuel Fangio in '57. As a result, Niki had dug deeper than he cared to do again. He spoke from rare experience when he called it "the ultimate madness." In his opinion, if you weren't frightened here, you weren't going fast enough.

His polling of fellow members of the Grand Prix Drivers' Association at its 1976 spring get-together—with a view to boycotting or relocating the German GP—had a cold logic to it: The Nürburgring was too long for it to be adequately marshaled and for acceptable medical cover to be guaranteed as opposed to airily promised; an ambulance could be many minutes distant.

Hunt was among those who agreed fundamentally with Lauda, but he was unwilling to renege on an agreed-upon three-year period of grace designed to allow its owners to complete the mammoth task of updating the circuit's safety features. This was the last year of that deal.

Lauda lost the vote, and considered his "opponents" either too brave or too stupid, or both.

Upon Lauda's arrival at the circuit, a fan, apparently without malice, shoved a photograph of Austria's 1970 World Champion Jochen Rindt's grave in his face. It was one stupid omen too many. After taking another pop at the facilities, and with accusations of cowardice ringing in his ears, he boarded his Ferrari, divorced himself from all negative thoughts, and set a qualifying time that only Hunt could beat. The Englishman, who had more reasons—23 net or 35 gross, depending on the outcome of the Brands Hatch protest—to shrug acceptance of the race's circumstances, expressed the usual Nürburgring mix of emotions: pride and relief. James had regularly reiterated that his vomiting was a necessary part of his ritual, a purging of emotion. On this occasion, however, he freely admitted to feeling frightened in the cockpit. He was glad to see the finish line at the end of each lap.

Tension before the start was as high as the clouds were low. One competitor wondered aloud if the organizers weren't waiting sadistically for the rain to begin before starting the GP. After a delay

----

OPPOSITE: The calm: Lauda—hand on gas cylinder, crash helmet casually placed on rear wing—chats as the mechanics go through their routine checks. The storm was yet to come.

of 30 minutes, it was officially declared a wet race. Tire choice, however, remained far from certain: It could be raining on one part of the circuit and be dry on another, variations of shade and breeze further complicating the equation of grip. Hunt considered fitting slicks before noticing that those around him on the grid were sitting on chunky wets. He had gambled in similar weather before a 1973 Formula 2 race here, and completed the first lap a very distant last. He decided to play it safe now that the stakes were so much higher. By no stretch of the imagination was he totally tally-ho.

The only man to gamble was Jochen Mass, Hunt's teammate. Mired on the fifth row, and desperate to kick-start his season, "Herman" resolutely stuck with slicks—a piece of blue-sky

----

OPPOSITE: Wooden gear knob, polished gear gate: classic Ferrari. Hip-hugging "bathtub": classic 1970s Formula 1. By this time the Scuderia felt confident enough to eradicate the stiffening tubes within its folded monocoque. Either way, however, a driver was afforded little protection. Also, note the offset angle of the steering column. It all seems so simplistic. What could possibly go wrong? **ABOVE:** His work done, chief mechanic Ermanno Cuoghi takes five on the 312 T2's left-front Goodyear prior to the race. The plethora of gaudy ski jackets indicates not only the fashion of the day but also its temperature. There was an ominously chill wind blowing.

thinking that lifted him to fourth by the first corner and into a commanding lead partway through the second lap.

Hunt and Lauda, who had made a particularly bad start, were among the 14 to peel in for new rubber at the end of the first lap. Niki reemerged clamped to the gearbox of Carlos Pace's Brabham-Alfa Romeo, and soon they were picking off the wet-shod backmarkers yet to pit.

Approaching the tight right at Bergwerk—scene of Lauda's 1973 twitch "warning"—the Ferrari snapped left, then speared right. It scythed through a line of wire catch-fencing and rebounded from the steep bank behind. This impact dragged its tail around and pitched the car into two clockwise rotations before coming to rest facing the oncoming traffic and minus its left-hand wheels. That side's rubber fuel cell had been torn off. Lauda was engulfed in flames.

The Hesketh of Guy Edwards managed to squeak past the stationary Ferrari, but Brett Lunger's Surtees could not, and punted it down the road, where they were impacted by Edwards's teammate, Harald Ertl. "Little Art" Merzario's Williams screeched to a halt just shy.

Lauda's "cavalry" had arrived.

Vietnam vet Lunger, who had received word of the death of his father only the day before, attempted to haul Lauda from the cockpit while Ertl thumped a fire extinguisher into smoky life. Precious seconds ticked by. Panic and adrenaline rising, Lunger swung his leg over in order to straddle the cockpit and continued to tug while Merzario reached into the 800-degree heat to undo Lauda's safety harness.

Click. The belts' sudden release caused Lunger to topple over—and mercifully Lauda shot out with him.

Those seconds had run to almost a minute.

- -

OPPOSITE: Clay Regazzoni consults with Goodyear's Leo Mehl, while teammate Lauda acquaints himself with the facts. Though Goodyear had a monopoly, the black art of finding well-matched sets of its cross-ply tires became paramount among teams and drivers, while the mixing of staggered diameter sizes further fogged the situation. It was by now becoming clear, however, that McLaren had stolen a march in such matters. **ABOVE:** Jochen Mass would make a splash by using his local knowledge and ditching his wet tires in favor of slicks before the first start. Nobody else took that gamble. (As an aside, this writer once heard Cosworth DFV engine designer Keith Duckworth bemoan the fact that Formula 1 teams made little or no effort to make the interiors of their air boxes as smooth as the exteriors.)

By the time his rescue helicopter had delivered him to Mannheim University Clinic, **Niki just wanted to sleep**, didn't want to know, and was thankful that it would soon all be over. Doctors feared the worst.

Niki walked to the edge of the track before his rescuers persuaded him to lie on the grass, where they divested him of his burned race suit and checked for broken bones. There were none that they could feel—he had in fact cracked some ribs, a cheekbone, and a collarbone—and John Watson, who had stopped his Penske ahead of the scene and was cradling Lauda's head in his lap, told Niki that his face was fine. Keeping him calm while waiting for the ambulance was the best they could do.

Where was that damn ambulance? According to Watson it took between five and six minutes to arrive.

Lauda's face wasn't fine, of course. His crash helmet had been tipped off his head and into his lap by the first impact, leaving him protected only by a flame-resistant balaclava. As a result, he had suffered burns of different degrees: His eyelids had fried, the top of his right ear had melted, and his scalp was charred. Severe rather than critical, these he could deal with, both now and in the future. It was what could not be seen that almost killed him.

Fumes from the burning petrol, melting bodywork, and deformable structure—a safety requirement within the car—and the extinguisher's halon had scorched his windpipe and poisoned his lungs. By the time his rescue helicopter had delivered him to Mannheim University Clinic, Niki just wanted to sleep, didn't want to know, and was thankful that it would soon all be over. Doctors feared the worst.

Hunt later explained that he knew little of this. By the time his McLaren rolled up to the roadblock, the cause of the red flags had been whirled away, and the secondhand info he could muster was hopeful: Lauda was walking and talking; his diagnosis was not serious, and there was no reason why he could not be mended and returned to action in two weeks. Thus Hunt lined up for the restart without alarm or qualm. He had a job to do. It was as simple—and as complicated—as that.

There was no repeat of the arguments that had blighted the British GP. This race was simply reset to zero, and no spare cars were allowed. Nor was there any debate about tires. Mass's patch of blue had proliferated, and a stiff northwester had dried the track. Slicks were universal, and

----

OPPOSITE: Lauda's wreckage is returned to the paddock. It would never be officially independently inspected.

poor Jochen, who had been ahead by 30 seconds by the end of the second lap, was dragged back into the midfield.

Having executed a good getaway at last, Hunt strung together his most aggressive lap of the season to forge a 9-second lead. Jody Scheckter gave chase in the six-wheeled Tyrrell, setting the fastest lap in the process, but James controlled their gap despite only receiving pit signals once every seven minutes. His hand no longer needed holding. He had passed his greatest examination with flying colors: He had gone solo. He was a World Champion in the making.

A delighted Teddy Mayer—McLaren did not have a good track record at the 'Ring—was beaming from ear to ear as a rightly satisfied Hunt stood on the podium alongside Scheckter and a rueful Mass. Hunt couldn't help but notice and respond in kind to his boss's grin. They would never again be simpatico.

Monday morning changed the mood. Lauda was close to death, and Hunt, so assuredly in command on Sunday, felt helpless and hopeless. He and Niki had long ago discussed just such a possibility, but still James felt underprepared for the shock of not just his friend's injuries, but also of the depth of their friendship: chasing girls, sinking beers, and tangling wheels had been, he realized now, the tip of their iceberg. He needed Niki. He didn't want to become World Champion while his main rival, at best, watched proceedings from a hospital bed or, at worst, lay in a grave. Though there was a selfish element to his reaction, it was genuine. The telegram he sent Lauda, lighthearted in tone, was compiled with a heavy heart.

Lauda was too ill for Hunt's well-meaning provocative message to have any effect. Rather, it was the doom-laden ministering of the last rites on Tuesday that tripped his survival switch. There had been some kind of mistake; he was not going to die! No matter how low his oxygen level was.

By Wednesday, he was breathing freely. On Thursday, he sat up in a chair. By Friday, he was discussing future race plans. By the time he had undergone the first of his many skin grafts the following week, he had decided that he would return to continue the defense of his title at the Canadian GP in early October.

Few believed him. Enzo Ferrari certainly didn't. After his team pronounced that its car had not been at fault in Germany, he set about locating a replacement for its driver. He found one in Carlos Reutemann, whose relationship with the Brabham team had hit rock bottom.

OPPOSITE: After his most efficient launch all year, Hunt begins his most impressive lap of the season, while those behind him begin the squabbling that will guarantee his swift, clean break. Clay Regazzoni (2) half-spun at Brünnchen, and Patrick Depailler (4) crashed in avoidance. Carlos Pace, obscured here, used this melee to slip through into second and hold up Jody Scheckter, Hunt's likeliest rival in the absence of Lauda, for a crucial period. And both Jochen Mass and Mario Andretti had grassy moments on the opening lap. Hunt's advantage by the end of it was nine seconds.

Lauda had **watched amateur footage of his accident with a dispassionate eye**, and although he was unable to absolve himself from blame, he could see no reason why the team felt that it could.

It had been bad enough when a visiting Emerson Fittipaldi revealed to Lauda that Ferrari had approached him with a view to signing a two-year contract with immediate effect. But Reutemann! Lauda couldn't stand the enigmatic, moody Argentinean—the feeling was mutual— and he brought forward his timetable in response to this "painful news," which was saying something, given his injuries. His revised due date was Monza in September.

Lauda had watched amateur footage of his accident with a dispassionate eye, and although he was unable to absolve himself from blame, he could see no reason why the team felt that it could. The crash occurred at a corner so nondescript in Nürburgring terms that it did not warrant a name: a 150 mph downhill left-handed kink that Lauda would reckon to take flat out even in the changeable conditions.

He surmised that the cause was a broken suspension component. The wreckage was never officially investigated, but Ermanno Cuoghi, Lauda's vastly experienced chief mechanic and close friend, admitted that he had been aware of failures of the left-rear magnesium tie rod. Indeed, he propounded this theory in the immediate aftermath. And yet the phrase "not tidy" was widely linked to Lauda's driving just prior to the accident. Though this was hardly surprising given the wet/dry track and resultant cold/hot tires, it felt like an allegation.

Whether the pointed adjectival phrase emanated from within or without, all trust between driver and team management had been erased. The only thing that continued to "unite" them was the contract Lauda had browbeaten from Enzo just days before the fire.

OPPOSITE (TOP): A somewhat somber podium—and this is before the seriousness of Lauda's injuries was known. The man in the gray sports jacket is Helmut Kohl. Then the minister-president of the Rhineland-Palatinate, he would go on to become German chancellor from 1982–98. The architect of Germany's reunification and co-founder of the European Union, he also knew the value of having his country's grand prix held on his local patch. **OPPOSITE (BOTTOM):** Hunt and Jody Scheckter are distracted, and Jochen Mass wonders (Doh!) what might have been but for Lauda's accident. "Herman" finished third from a mid-grid slot, but he'd had the first race "won" when it was halted. The 77 on the famous electronic scoreboard indicates track specialist Rolf Stommelen's sixth place. He had been scheduled to race a year-old Brabham for the RAM team, but when the car was impounded after Friday practice by a court injunction, he was offered the third works BT45. His performance was historically significant because it marked the debut of a Formula 1 car featuring carbon-fiber brake discs.

CHAPTER 6

Yes, Catching Niki

I t should have been easier without Lauda.

It wasn't.

Not only was Hunt faced with a new prospect of being expected to win, but also several rivals, sensing their chance—one was easier to beat than two—stepped forward to fill the gap left by Niki. These included John Watson, Ronnie Peterson, Jody Scheckter and Patrick Depailler, Jacques Laffite, and Mario Andretti and Gunnar Nilsson. Whereas Ferrari had begun to mark time in terms of development, Penske, March, Tyrrell, Ligier, and Lotus were yomping along. The grid closed up as a consequence, and the next two grands prix provided something the Hunt-Lauda battle hadn't: frenetic back-and-forth dicing. Watching on television, Lauda suddenly saw the big picture. He could only hope that his team had spotted it also.

OPPOSITE: No fun without Niki. Hunt weathers an Austrian storm. It rained on both days of practice, but not before Hunt had claimed another pole position in a dry first session. **ABOVE:** Details. Because Hunt was so tall, his windscreen had to be raised to protect him from buffeting. The colorful stripes on his crash helmet were those of his alma mater, Wellington College.

Why should he be enjoying life when **his friend was living their worst nightmare?** The extended phone conversations between them were packed with macho gallows humor and linked by a whispered thread of fate: When might Hunt's luck run out?

That was a forlorn hope. Instead, Ferrari retreated to its fortress. Enzo had announced his withdrawal from motor racing. Forever. Again. His ire at the off-track decisions that had denied his team two victories was understandable even to McLaren's Teddy Mayer, but Ferrari's absence from the Österreichring was seen for what it was: petulant and cynical. Its efforts—clandestine to begin with—to get Lauda's home race canceled was its way of "respecting" its wounded number one, of "acting in his best interests." Lauda was as unconvinced by this as everybody else. He, too, saw a Scuderia suddenly riven by insecurity and paranoia and reverting to type.

Hunt was in a compromised mood, too, his need to win tempered by guilt. Why should he be enjoying life when his friend was living their worst nightmare? The extended phone conversations between them were packed with macho gallows humor and linked by a whispered thread of fate: When might Hunt's luck run out?

Again he was at his calmest within the claustrophobic confines of the M23's cockpit. The Austrian Grand Prix was the most competitive of the season to date, with some of the closest racing seen for years, and James was too busy to stew. Watson led to begin with, his Penske PC4 having followed McLaren's route of a longer wheelbase with skirts. Then Peterson hustled by in his slippery March. Then a charging Scheckter hit the front for a lap. Then Ronnie led for another lap. By which time the sun had dried the track and a composed Watson promptly made the decisive move that would bring his and Penske's first GP victory.

Hunt, who had started from pole position, was battling with understeer that had set in before he ran over the muck and debris from Scheckter's huge five-working-wheels accident on lap 15. Laffite (Ligier) and Nilsson (Lotus) passed the McLaren on their way to second and third places before its driver could recalibrate his style. When Hunt did so, he set the race's fastest lap to finish a close fourth. His mechanics later discovered that his left-front airfoil had been knocked askew and its underside holed. Hunt impressed them more and more.

OPPOSITE: Hunt, both front wings damaged, fends off Mario Andretti's Lotus 77 on the run to the first corner at the Österreichring. They would finish fourth and fifth, respectively.

The Dutch GP at Zandvoort, with its top 14 qualifiers separated by less than a second, was another thriller, filled with Formula 3-type antics. School, it seemed, was out for the summer. Ferrari, as anticipated, returned albeit with a single car for Regazzoni, but it was Watson who again took the fight to Hunt and McLaren—albeit after another spurt from Peterson.

The svelte Penske was clearly the fastest car on the track—but Hunt was the smartest driver. Despite yet more understeer on full tanks, he was sufficiently close to take advantage of a botched attempted pass of Peterson by Watson to grab second place. A few laps later he dived by Ronnie for the lead when the Swede slid wide on oil. Thereafter he spent 20 or so laps fending off Watson, making the most of a fractional speed advantage along the main straight and showing his rival only the outside of the banked Tarzan corner.

The pressure didn't stop when a bearing in the Penske's gearbox failed on lap 47. Regazzoni, spiked into action by the jinking attentions of Andretti's Lotus 77, began to close on a McLaren further hampered by a brake air-scoop that had worked loose and was thus disrupting the airflow over its front wing. Had it not been for some judicious lapping of

backmarkers, Hunt might not have won on his 29th birthday. He was now within two points of Lauda—and Enzo had marked Regazzoni's card for failing to win at a circuit that was historically suited to Ferraris.

The points gap was extended to five at Monza, where Hunt was full of admiration for his mate's heroic return, and full of contempt for what he saw as Italy's biased media and blinkered fans, conniving Ferrari and complicit officials. Any comparisons with what had happened at Brands Hatch were absurd. In his opinion.

OPPOSITE: A wreathed and smiling John Watson celebrates his maiden Formula 1 victory. He was joined on the podium at the Österreichring by (left) runner-up Jacques Laffite—after scoring his best result of the season for Ligier—and Lotus's Gunnar Nilsson. Most notably, however, it would appear that "Marilyn Monroe" had made a surprise appearance in Austria. **ABOVE:** (From left to right) Arturo Merzario, a German marshal, Harald Ertl, and Brett Lunger are honored for their bravery in rescuing Lauda at the Nürburgring. They received their awards at the Österreichring. Guy Edwards, the other member of the "crash team," was not present at this race, but would later collect a Queen's Gallantry Medal.

With a whiff of opposite lock, Hunt at his very best leans on the M23 at Zandvoort. Aerodynamic side skirts would not form a consistent seal against a track's surface until Dr. Harvey Postlethwaite, Hunt's former designer at Hesketh Racing, invented

His mood changed again when the gap was widened to 17 by the FIA. Its Court of Appeal chose not to believe McLaren's witnesses to the fact that Hunt was running when the red flags were shown at Brands. It handed the win to Lauda and confirmed Hunt's disqualification.

James was playing squash in Canada when he heard the news; Niki, head bandaged, was in Paris: different courts, different priorities and methods. McLaren could not be dissuaded from its belief that Lauda had won a sympathy vote. (Perhaps human weakness did have its uses.)

Hunt's fury was compounded when he read quotes attributed to Lauda stating that Niki was "delighted" by the ruling, and that justice had been done. James fired back a televisual volley that owed all to perceived treason and naught to received reason.

When the teams bumped into each other at the Flying Dutchman Hotel, near Mosport, northeast of Toronto, the olive branch, already bending, was snapped: Ferrari team manager Daniele Audetto was told to get lost, and Lauda was curtly informed that Hunt did not want to be part of the flaring debate about this fast and sweeping circuit's safety facilities.

Hunt would eventually attempt to explain his actions as kidology, an effort to freak out Ferrari and Lauda—not that they needed any more reason. There can be no denying, however, that his attitude blackened and his behavior became more outlandish and boorish after the shine had been taken from the increasingly distant glittering prize of the World Championship. It was a disillusioned Hunt that went on a sex-and-booze bender in Canada.

He had favorably surprised McLaren so often that it just let him get on with it—and even covered for him on occasion. This supposedly uptight team was in fact more *laissez-faire* than freewheelin' Hesketh Racing, where "Bubbles" Horsley had acted as Hunt's housemaster, headmaster, and taskmaster. James appreciated the extra freedom at McLaren, and the implied trust, and responded for the most part in good faith and with professionalism. When the balance suddenly skewed, however, the team had neither the knowledge, nor will, nor time to level with its driver.

Not that it mattered—Hunt drove like an angel all weekend: victory from pole position, despite arriving on the grid with a devil of a hangover and after a dalliance with a local pop star. Once again, the M23 was his source of genuine contentment. He had never enjoyed himself so much behind the wheel. And by common consent, he had never driven better.

Peterson's March again blasted into a short-lived lead followed by a long-term battle with understeer, and this time it was Depailler who took the fight to Hunt, his six-wheeler appearing

----

OPPOSITE: A cloth and a clipboard protect Hunt from splashes while his M23 is refueled in Holland. McLaren's Nicholson-tuned Cosworth DFV was reckoned to give a maximum of 6.5 mpg, and 42 gallons of tankage was reckoned sufficient to get the car to the finish of any grand prix without stopping.

Although his outlook meant that he needed Hunt less than James needed him, he realized that **they were to be forever intertwined in history**, and that one without the other was a lesser man.

to have more front-end grip than a McLaren that was hampered by a tad of oversteer. With a potentially faster car filling his mirrors, James once more made expert use of lapped cars, slowing down or speeding up in order to pass them where they would give the chasing Frenchman the biggest headache. This battle lasted until gas fumes from a leaking fuel-pressure gauge caused Patrick a genuine headache. He was on the verge of collapse by the finish.

Hunt, eight points in arrears with two rounds remaining, continued to underplay his chances of winning the title. He might have considered this defeatist a few years before; now he was simply being rational. He'd learned from Lauda.

At Watkins Glen, Hunt embarked in a fantastic race-long dice with Scheckter. Another rival with a sharp mind and a prickly relationship with the media, it's little wonder that Jody was on James's list of good guys. Right now, though, he was standing in the way of his dream. Hunt again profited from wayward backmarkers to take the lead from the Tyrrell on lap 37 (of 59), only to lose it four laps later when he, too, was balked, and missed a gear. He was not to be denied; he had to win. That was as clear as the autumnal New England light.

He was back ahead by lap 46—a strong move that required no help from others—and reeled off a sequence of stunning laps to ensure victory. His fastest lap undercut his pole time, and although five others achieved this unusual feat, none could get within 0.27 seconds of Hunt's best.

Early in the race, Hunt had given himself a talking-to because he felt as though he were "driving like a grandmother." It took him five laps of self-help before he deemed his concentration and accuracy commensurate with the demands of his situation. As such, he felt that his development as a world-class driver had turned yet another corner.

It had.

Which of them was "The Computer" now?

Hunt had six wins to Lauda's five, eight poles to his three. He had overcome mechanical and philosophical problems, plus emotional and mental blocks, to beat faster cars, and had salvaged

OPPOSITE: Birthday boy Hunt—he was 29—looks thoughtful after winning the Dutch Grand Prix for a second consecutive year. Clay Regazzoni (left) and Mario Andretti join him on the podium. This trio was separated by a tick more than two seconds after 75 laps of frantic action.

ABOVE: Watson hounds Hunt but fails to outfox him. The 33-lap battle for the lead between these UK racers was the best dice of the season so far. Penske's PC4 was the faster car—particularly when one of the McLaren's front-brake cooling ducts worked loose and started to disrupt the airflow over the car. **OPPOSITE:** Jochen Mass takes note while his M26 is fettled. The German concentrated on McLaren's new design in Holland (well, he wasn't going to beat Hunt in M23s). Its tricky handling was blamed on the revised positioning of the rear anti-rollbar. Whatever the cause, the M26 was pointy and unpredictable, whereas the M23 was pliant and adaptable. Mass stuck to his guns and qualified 15th—having crashed because of a broken driveshaft—and struggled to 9th place after a spin in the race. Lapped by the victorious M23, it was a disappointing debut for this car.

what he could on the occasions that he could not. Apart from at Monza, he had driven like a champion. (And there were extenuating circumstances on that occasion.)

Were he to become World Champion, he would be deserving of the accolade.

Lauda could see that. Although his outlook meant that he needed Hunt less than James needed him, he realized that they were to be forever intertwined in history, and that one without the other was a lesser man. Hunt concurred. Together they rose above the squabbles. They met, made amends, and shook hands after the Canadian GP. Their falling-out was a natural consequence of the arena they found themselves in. Indeed, they did well to keep personal politics out of it for as long as they had. That they were then able to erase them so quickly was indicative of the strength of their bond. It could not be broken, no matter how loudly the front pages shouted.

The air between them cleared, the FIA's paper trail thankfully at an end, they both knew at last exactly where they stood and what they needed to do at the final round to become the World Champion.

The gap was three points in Lauda's favor.

OPPOSITE: The shine on boss Roger Penske's shoes matches the immaculate finish of his team's PC4. Look at the size of those chromed front suspension rockers! In the background is the Ligier pit. The team's drivers, John Watson and Jacques Laffite, would both retire from the Dutch Grand Prix at Zandvoort. **ABOVE:** March's Ronnie Peterson again grabs the lead at the start in Canada while teammate Vittorio Brambilla attempts to squeeze between Hunt and the pit wall. "Superswede" would lead for eight laps before a blistered right-front tire and fading brakes—a regular problem with the Formula 2–based 761—plunged him to an eventual ninth place. "The Monza Gorilla," meanwhile, spent the latter half of the race having to hold his lever in fourth gear and eventually slipped to 14th.

CHAPTER 7

Dead Man Racing

His presence in Monza's paddock was met by disbelief, dismay, and even disgust. Universal acceptance of the heroism of his decision and actions would come later. Lurid headlines about Lauda's disfigurement had "prepared" the world for the worst, and, right now, many found it hard to look him in the face—and not just because he wore a red baseball cap pulled low and large sunglasses despite a slate-gray sky to protect his injuries from the elements and straining lenses.

This was embarrassing for Enzo Ferrari and Carlos Reutemann. The former could not be blamed for bolstering his beleaguered team—though his handling of the situation was typically

---

OPPOSITE: Hunt emphatically makes his point to an unmoved Lauda. There can be no doubt that the intimidating atmosphere at Monza unsettled the temperamental Englishman. Despite his bad-boy image, he didn't like being the bad guy. After his first-lap accident in the wet Friday-morning practice, he attempted to whip up a motion to have the session stopped, to no avail. Although an unnerved Lauda was seeking any excuse not to get into his Ferrari, he had no desire to show any sign of weakness. **ABOVE:** Hunt at Parabolica, the final long right-hander before the pit straight. The bulge in the cockpit side that caused the Marlboro wording to distort was to allow room for Hunt to operate the gear lever. The M23's gearbox, a Hewland, featured six forward ratios. All the other teams bar Brabham made do with five.

Both Friday practice sessions were very wet, and Lauda used every excuse in the book to climb from the car. **He was scared rigid, and drove accordingly.** He was in need of a reboot.

insensitive—nor could the latter be criticized for accepting Enzo's offer. Like the rest of the world, they had not expected Lauda to return so soon. If at all. Just 39 days and nights had passed since his accident—yet here he was. Ferrari's garage, therefore, was cramped, filled with awkward silences and furtive glances.

L auda was playing it tough while planning to follow comfortingly familiar routines: objective, rational, and systematic. Although observers doubted he was physically and/or mentally ready to return, the man himself felt sure he would be able to cope. Austrian fitness guru Willi Dungl, whom Lauda met in the aftermath of the tractor shunt, had worked wonders with a broken body.

The mind, however, was more difficult to assess and to fix. Up rushed jangling nerves, a pounding heart, and all that a churning stomach brings. "The Computer" was human. Hunt had been "Lauda" in Niki's absence; now Lauda was "Hunt."

Both Friday practice sessions were very wet, and Lauda used every excuse in the book to climb from the car. He was scared rigid, and drove accordingly. He was in need of a reboot.

During a reflective night at his hotel, Lauda realized that he had been trying too hard, too soon. Like his team, he had felt insecure, and overreacted as a result. On Saturday, he let it come to him, worked up to it, and qualified fifth, two places ahead of—and fully 0.29 seconds quicker than—Reutemann, and four places ahead of Regazzoni. This was sufficient to convince him that his skills were intact and confirm his fear that Ferrari had let its test-and-development program slip while he was recuperating. (Ahead of him on the grid at this renowned power circuit were 12-cylinders from Alfa Romeo and Matra.)

The Scuderia had invested time and effort on its politicking against McLaren when it should have been looking within. The uncomfortable truths were that Hunt and the M23 were better than

----

OPPOSITE: Shadowy men keep a beady eye on a Shadow. Monza's "security guards" had a distinct air of militia about them. The phrase "It takes one to catch one" springs to mind.

Three's a crowd in the Ferrari pit. A wry Lauda eavesdrops on a Carlos Reutemann conversation. The latter was impressed by the 312 T2's engine and gearbox, but its cockpit was too small for him, and he suffered cramps in the latter stages of the grand prix, sliding down the order to an eventual ninth, having run as high as fifth. He would have to wait until January 1977 for his next race with the Scuderia. Graffiti in a garage is a definite no-no in today's sanitized Formula 1.

it had imagined and were improving with every race, and that McLaren was a purposeful team with an inclusive pull-together ethos.

The latter was placed under extreme stress at Monza. McLaren had anticipated tit-for-tat at the home of Ferrari, and had departed early from the UK in case persnickety border officials held them up. They did.

As the *capo* of the English Formula 1 mafia, Hunt was hardly likely to be welcomed at Monza; the *tifosi* had its own Mafia, thank you very much. Consequently, he was jostled, booed, hissed, and spat at by tribal spectators who threw stones at his car and gleefully received his nose-bashing spin at the Parabolica on the first lap of practice.

Given the pervading air of suspicion, McLaren felt the need to fence its area of the paddock (an unfortunate precedent). Also, it made every effort to be squeaky-clean. Rumor was rife that it was using illegal fuel to boost performance. Methanol, chosen because of its use in Indy Car racing, was stored in the pressure bottle ostensibly used to "ignite" the onboard pneumatic starter. Or so the story went. It came as no surprise when McLaren's fuel supplier Texaco was also held at the border.

Random samples were collected on Saturday and taken for analysis. On the morning of the race it was announced that those of McLaren and Penske (American by name, but based in Dorset, England) were illegal, and that these teams had been disqualified as a result.

There was an anomaly in the rules. Teams were allowed to use the highest octane rating commercially available in their country of origin, plus a one-point tolerance. Britain's highest was 101. But when the meeting's officials checked with the CSI, they were informed erroneously that the permitted universally available maximum was 100—mainland Europe's highest. McLaren's had been measured at 101.6—Texaco test-rated it at 101.2—and Penske's at an unbelievable 105.7. Lotus and Tyrrell were deemed legal, while Ferrari's result was a conservative—or forewarned—98.6.

After much argument, the penalty was amended: Their times from Saturday's drying, faster practice session were rescinded instead. This meant that Hunt, Jochen Mass, and John Watson would start from the back of the 26-car grid, and then only because two others had been persuaded to withdraw, and overawed Tyrrell privateer Otto Stuppacher had returned to Vienna, convinced that he had failed to qualify.

Hunt considered not taking the start in an understeering car that he was unhappy with in any case. (His best time would have been good enough for ninth on the grid.) That, however, would

----

OPPOSITE: Hunt discusses tires with Goodyear's competitions guru, Leo Mehl. Both practice sessions on Friday were held in cool, wet conditions.

have heaped more embarrassment on Texaco, as well as being detrimental to his championship hopes and disrespectful to his friend Lauda. Instead, he drove a furious race that harked back to his formative days.

Niki's return had unsettled everybody.

Quelling qualifying nerves had been one thing. The thought of barreling into the new first chicane surrounded by an unflinching pack sniffing for weakness was quite another. Niki was sitting in neutral and watching for the 10-second board when the lights flashed green prematurely. He completed the first lap in 12th place. His subsequent race would be a model of control.

Hunt completed the first lap in 24th place, having failed to benefit from the rolling start that those toward the rear of the lineup had been afforded by the starter's twitchy index finger. Mass, for example, made up 10 places from 25th.

Hunt's charge began on the second lap. He was determined to take every opportunity to pass in the first half of the race, with a view to settling down in the second and hopefully picking up some points with a top-six finish. By lap 10 (of 52), he had risen to 12th place.

ABOVE: Abuse with a handy translation. This fan had no time for the rule-makers either: vergogna means shame.

OPPOSITE: Organizers obtain a fuel sample from Penske before Saturday's practice sessions. The Poole-based team's Sunoco brew from America was "measured" in a Milan laboratory at 105.7 octane, the strongest of the lot.

James was surprisingly tolerant of the marshals who prevented his climbing back into the beached car after a quick inspection of it, but he **seemed prepared to take on the baiting crowd**, and not necessarily one at a time.

Jacky Ickx's Ensign was his next target, but he missed a gear when the Belgian caused him to check at the first chicane, and this allowed Tom Pryce's Shadow to draw level on the long run to the next chicane. Hunt had no wish to pass the late-braking Welshman for a second time, and so decided to sit it out on the outside of the first part of the complex. Although there was no contact between the cars, Hunt missed his braking point and the McLaren slid wide and sank into the sand short of the catch-fencing.

James was surprisingly tolerant of the marshals who prevented his climbing back into the beached car after a quick inspection of it, but he seemed prepared to take on the baiting crowd, and not necessarily one at a time. In his defense, the hostile reaction he received on his long walk to the sanctuary of his garage was indefensible. Ferrari team manager Daniele Audetto said the anger was directed at McLaren rather than its driver. Easy to say when you're not on the receiving end.

Upon his return, Hunt harshly labeled Pryce "absolutely brainless." In a much later, quieter, calmer moment, James would admit that he had been at fault, but still felt he had been in a position that left him no option other than to fight back. He reckoned it a calculated risk.

Lauda was, understandably, even more calculating, particularly after he had spotted his rival's parked car. Even so, he picked off hard men Mario Andretti (Lotus) and Vittorio Brambilla (March), the unpredictable Hans Stuck (March), the ailing Tyrrells of Jody Scheckter and Patrick Depailler, and—most satisfactory of all—Reutemann. He increased his pace throughout the race and twice held its fastest lap, including when seven laps from home; only podium finishers Ronnie Peterson (March), teammate Regazzoni, and Jacques Laffite (Ligier) lapped faster. His oil pressure began to sag with three laps to go, but he was able to fend off Scheckter to finish a magnificent fourth.

OPPOSITE: Hunt for James. The Lotus 77s of Gunnar Nilsson and Mario Andretti lead the rear half of the grid through the new double chicane after the start. Against expectation everybody made it through intact. Vittorio Brambilla's March (9) would come closest to scoring a point on the day; he finished seventh. Tom Pryce (16) was to finish eighth in the Shadow DN8 that indirectly caused Hunt's retirement.

On the warpath. Hunt trudges to the pits after sliding off the track at the second chicane. He received a hostile reception from a jubilant crowd, and although he would occasionally pause to goad the fans, he was genuinely relieved to reach his garage unscathed. One of his well-aimed punches would have started a riot on this occasion.

Lauda was sore and absolutely drained. His fire-resistant balaclava was soaked in blood, despite adaptations to his distinctive AGV crash helmet, and slivers of skin came with it as he peeled it from his head. Jackie Stewart called it the bravest sporting comeback he'd ever witnessed. The man whose clinical approach to winning had not sat well with Ferrari's passionate fans was cheered to the echo. As he did at Brands Hatch, he paid hysteria little heed. Just two days before, it had been directed against him. If people considered his actions somehow disrespectful or his form repellent, or thought that his swift return lacked dignity, it was of no concern to him. He had enough on his plate without it. Any satisfaction he felt came from within.

- -

ABOVE: Ferrari's latest recruit, Carlos Reutemann (his nickname was "Lole"), has support in the admittedly ad hoc grandstands. Advertising hoardings were butchered by fans that were desperate for a better view. **OPPOSITE:** Now and forever! Hepped-up tifosi show their allegiance at the circuit gates. Vittorio Brambilla never drove for Ferrari (his elder brother Tino did), but the March driver was a Monza native. Arturo Merzario was born in Civenna on the western shore of Lake Como in the far north of the country; he had, however, driven for Ferrari in Formula 1 and sports-car racing. Note that there had been no time to add the flag of Argentina to the left-hand banner to mark the arrival of Reutemann at Ferrari.

HUNT VS. LAUDA

In contrast, although Hunt possessed an uncanny knack for upsetting people and tended to act in haste and repent at leisure, he was not preternaturally disposed to playing the villain. His swagger was a cover. What people thought about him mattered to him, and he admitted to being upset by this "very heavy deal" at Monza. He had arrived two points behind Lauda, having finished the same number of races, and should have consolidated. Instead he drove on negative emotion and paid a personal price.

Two weeks later, the FIA found against him with respect to the British Grand Prix, and in the next breath admitted that its Monza fuel ruling was incorrect, and its testing methods inadequate. McLaren and Texaco were absolved. There was no comfort in that, but there was in the knowledge that the worst was over—that Monza was behind them. Hunt had been relieved to escape unharmed, and was proud at how the team had responded to provocation—and ultimately been vindicated. That they had scored no points was almost irrelevant.

Lauda, too, was relieved to escape Monza, albeit for different reasons. He had—for now—conquered his demons. Now it was his team's turn. What Niki wanted from it was composure and continuity, for a pragmatic line to be picked up and consistently followed. Having searched in vain for it at Monza, he was not looking forward to the long haul to North America.

As anticipated, his 312 T2 was not quite at the races. He struggled with it over the Mosport bumps, qualified sixth, and was running fifth at three-quarter distance when worsening but manageable oversteer veered out of control. His rear-suspension mounting had failed. Lauda lost three places within two laps, and eighth he remained. Given what had happened in Germany, it's a wonder that he pressed on to the finish.

Watkins Glen was a bit better, but still he was no match for an inspired Hunt. He finished third more than a minute in arrears.

On the morning of that race he had rudely awoken his rival by bursting through their adjoining door at the Glen Motor Inn already dressed in his racing overalls. He stood to attention over James's bed and pronounced: "Today I vin ze championship!"

It was a joke cracked more in hope than expectation.

OPPOSITE: Lauda and Ferrari team manager Daniele Audetto stand shoulder to shoulder before the drivers' parade at Mosport in Canada. Theirs, however, was a strained relationship by this point. Lauda felt that his team manager had not given him sufficient support during the Reutemann Affair. Certainly, the ex-rally man was unable to fill Luca di Montezemolo's sizable shoes, but nor was he dealt an easy hand by circumstance. Lauda was not sorry to see him replaced for 1977. His relationship with successor Roberto Nosetto, however, was even worse. As an aside, how would the Ferrari of today view its number-one driver being ushered around a packed grand prix venue in a Porsche?

CHAPTER 8

You've Done It!

Barry Sheene was irreverent, handsome, and hot news. He knew exactly what Hunt was going through and how he liked to play it. Britain's newly crowned 500cc world motorcycle champion also knew exactly what Lauda was experiencing. "Sheeney" also had recently cheated death in a 170 mph crash, and stuff that had never bothered him before now played on his mind. He could see no reason why Niki wouldn't be feeling the same way.

Physical recovery was the easy bit.

Sheene, who was in Japan for a meeting with his Suzuki paymasters, detoured to Fuji International Raceway to provide moral (and immoral) support to his mate, James, who had been in Japan for a fortnight. Ostensibly Hunt was there to test at a circuit that was new to the calendar, and to him. Alastair Caldwell had freighted an M23 directly from Watkins Glen against

---

OPPOSITE: As the mist rolls back to reveal a portion of Mount Fuji, Hunt leads Jochen Mass in a McLaren 1-2 at the first turn. The latter might have won this race had his concentration not slipped while riding shotgun to his team leader on lap 35. He had the faster car/tire combination, but by this stage of the season was willing to help his teammate become World Champion. (The spectators got a raw deal at this venue, by the way.) **ABOVE:** Marlboro men: Sheene and Hunt indulge in product placement.

The **Hunt-Lauda battle had blurred boundaries.**
James appeared on front covers of magazines because of the life he led off the track; Niki was on them because of his near-death experience on it.

the wishes of team boss Teddy Mayer and a gentleman's agreement with Ferrari. Tough "Guv" reckoned that any testing done more than a week before a race broke no "rule."

Delays at customs, problems with the car, and bad weather severely restricted Hunt's running, but Caldwell reckoned the trip worthwhile because his star driver had become fully oriented with the place and relaxed in his inimitable way. When Hunt wasn't beating all comers on the hotel's squash court, he was hitting on the latest harem of flight attendants to have jetted in. It beat jogging.

Lauda turned up low-key and tired. The strain was showing. The adrenaline that carried him through Monza had drained away in North America, and he was running on empty. While team manager Daniele Audetto attempted to stir up anger and opposition to McLaren's "illegal" testing, and demanded extra practice time for Ferrari, his star driver looked the other way and wished it over. He was sick of the press intrusion, sick of Enzo and his minions, and sick of a season in its 10th month.

The Hunt-Lauda battle had blurred boundaries. James appeared on front covers of magazines because of the life he led off the track; Niki was on them because of his near-death experience on it. When combined, and in very different ways, they had made the World Championship a truly global event—and neither was comfortable with the side effects of this. Party animal Hunt often felt lonely in a crowd, and clung tenaciously to his non-motor-racing friends. Like Hunt, Lauda had endured a socially chilly childhood. Unlike Hunt, he made no pretense at bonhomie. Take me and/or leave me was their shared credo. To which a voracious, tenacious press no longer paid heed.

Friday's practice sessions came as blessed relief for these racers: alone and, in theory, in control. Both battled handling problems on the softer, stickier tires that Goodyear had made available to its faster teams because of the presence of Bridgestone and Dunlop on some one-off Japanese entries. The Ferrari's front suspension had been altered to provide more camber compensation to work the tires harder and thus generate more heat in them, yet still it

----

OPPOSITE: Hunt, Lauda, Bernie Ecclestone, and Ronnie Peterson share a brolly—but not the same opinions. Ecclestone—though he looks chilled here—knew how important it was for the future of Formula 1 that its newfound global TV audience, drawn in by the Hunt/Lauda epic, was not left high and dry because of a start postponed by rain.

understeered. Hunt complained of a lack of traction and also understeer, and they finished the day separated by one-hundredth of a second on a provisional third row. This was more of a worry for the notoriously slow-starting Hunt who, in most people's estimation (including his own), needed to win the race to win the title.

Both improved on Saturday: Hunt to second on the grid, and Lauda to third, the gap between them extended to three-tenths. James's mood was thus much improved. Lauda's remained the same.

And then it rained. And rained. And rained some more.

The storm that swept in from China a day later than forecast was the last thing Lauda wanted. Another burden, another element out of his hands. Cloying mist shrouded the distant snowcapped summit of sacred Mount Fuji—it bestowed good fortune when visible—and Niki felt hemmed in by happenstance.

Not that Hunt was enamored with the situation either. He and Lauda spoke privately and agreed to attempt to get the race postponed—albeit not before James had stressed that he would take the start if it came to it, and race as hard as Lauda "forced" him to.

The drivers' Safety Committee and the team principals met with the organizers to argue their divergent cases. Much more than the drivers' World Championship was at stake. (Ferrari had been confirmed as the champion constructor at Watkins Glen.) Brabham team owner Bernie Ecclestone, kingpin of FOCA, had worked unrelentingly behind the scenes to unlock the East Asian market. With the world at last watching—via very expensive satellite links—a postponement or, worse, a cancellation would be catastrophic, and would delay his expansion plan by several years. He knew what he had in Hunt versus Lauda—TV gold that had to be cashed in when the market was buoyant, i.e., here and now.

So tensions mounted during a 90-minute delay. The sport's lack of an obvious leader, and the battle lines that such situations always drew up between the drivers and their teams, resulted in an argumentative fog that left uncoached spectators in the impending dark. They could go whistle. Which is exactly what they did when, at the devious behest of Caldwell, McLaren mechanic Lance Gibbs conducted them using a referee's Acme Thunderer and slow

---

OPPOSITE: Nicotine and caffeine are on Hunt's menu as he stalks the pit lane alongside British bike ace, Barry Sheene. The latter had recently been crowned as the 500cc World Champion for the first time. He achieved this with Suzuki despite absenting himself from the Isle of Man TT races, which he felt were too dangerous. Having won five of the six rounds he contested—he finished runner-up in the one he didn't win—he was also able to skip the final three rounds at "unfit" tracks: Imatra in Finland, Brno in Warsaw Pact Czechoslovakia—both road circuits—and the Nürburgring. Like Hunt, he had his own way of doing things.

hand-clapping gestures. As "riots" go, it was more orderly than that of Brands Hatch, but even more unexpected in so mannered a society.

The potential loss of honor that this reaction signaled, plus a few drivers' crossing of the picket line—Lauda's teammate Clay Regazzoni among them—caused a decision to be made: The race would start, albeit after a further five-minute delay.

Hunt, who had been gagging, hacking, and retching more violently than ever, and distractedly had taken a pee in full sight of the spectators—cue polite applause—walked a plank laid across one of the large puddles on the wide main straight and stepped aboard his M23. Ensconced, he tipped his helmet back against its roll hoop and closed his eyes. Lauda, crushed by all that had gone before, hunched forward in his Ferrari. Both knew that fate was about to be sorely tempted.

Unusually, Hunt got a good start, and while the rest pecked cautiously in his rooster tails, he skimmed and skittered to a huge lead by the end of the first lap. He was out of sight both

OPPOSITE: Jochen Mass stands beneath an umbrella in front of Fuji's rudimentary pits, while McLaren's stripy tarpaulin has another outing and shelters the German's M23. Note how the car's tires are exposed to the cold and damp weather. Rubber in heated blankets were a thing of Formula 1's future. Mass had qualified on the sixth row of the grid—1.25 seconds slower than Hunt—but would run strongly in the early stages of the race. **ABOVE:** A blinding start. Pedal to the metal despite the puddles, Hunt holds a huge advantage at the end of the first lap. Just visible in his spray is John Watson's Penske. Seconds later, the latter slithered up the escape road at the first corner and dropped seven places. He would eventually retire because of the team's second blown engine of the weekend.

To this day he does not reproach himself **about his decision to withdraw from the Japanese Grand Prix.** Why should he? It was braver than even his decision to race in Italy.

physically and metaphorically. Cautious Lauda, meanwhile, was drowning in the pack, unable to blink because of his injuries and questioning his sanity. He formulated his answer by lap two.

The number-one Ferrari, which felt like "a paper boat in a storm," rolled into the pits and drew up at its garage. Measured. The team descended upon it while Mauro Forghieri craned into its cockpit to ascertain the problem. (The spectating Sheene could have told him in a heartbeat.) The staring eyes that met Mauro's told him. A shrug from Niki confirmed it.

Lauda had a battle with his fear at Monza, not the war. Now it had returned stronger, and Niki unclicked his belts and disembarked. He had the skill but not the will to continue. It was "murder" out there. This wasn't racing, this was existing. Life was for living—and not just on the King's Road.

The team immediately reckoned to construct a cover story to protect his reputation. Once again it had read him wrong. Lauda had nothing to hide, and he told them so. To this day he does not reproach himself about his decision to withdraw from the Japanese Grand Prix. Why should he? It was braver than even his decision to race in Italy.

That's not to say he didn't curse his luck. He sat quietly on the pit counter for a few moments before wandering over to the pit wall, helmet off, cap on, overalls unzipped, to see how his title hung in the air. His friend James—the man he wanted to have it if he couldn't—was still leading. Niki would happily congratulate him if he won. But not here. He slipped into his civvies and headed for the Tokyo airport.

By which time Mount Fuji was peeking through a smear of blue. Against all expectation the weather had turned, and Lauda realized that if he had toughed it out for another 20 laps . . . But no, that wasn't the point. He would not beat himself up. The Italian media would do that for him: yellow man in a red-blooded car.

Hunt, pressing on as a driver without a world title must, managed to avoid the spinning March of Vittorio Brambilla, the "Monza Gorilla," driving as though it were a summer's day in Lombardy.

OPPOSITE (TOP): Everybody at Ferrari has "something more important to do" as Lauda steps from his perfectly sound 312 T2 and away from his World Championship bid. Only the rooftop cameraman grabbing the scoop was willing to front up to this sensational but awkward moment. **OPPOSITE (BOTTOM):** Lauda looks apprehensive. His race may be over, but the world drivers' title still hangs in the mist. He watched from the pit wall for several laps before slipping away quietly.

Much to McLaren's consternation, however, Hunt was also avoiding the puddles. Seeking them out would have cooled his soft-treaded tires and increased their life in the drying atmosphere, as a breeze had sprung up. The team hung out a beseeching signal to this effect. A clear, ready-made signal, not a scrawled chalk message—there's that attention to detail again—but Hunt was concentrating so fiercely as to be oblivious.

He did notice that his tires were deteriorating and cursed his team's indecision. The arrow it displayed was a question mark as far as he was concerned. It had the information about wear rates. Why couldn't they act on it? "Bubbles" would have.

In fact, said arrow was the agreed-upon symbol for "We are ready; pit when you are." After all, only James knew the state of his tires. Why couldn't he act on it? Emerson would have. (The Brazilian with two world titles in his pocket already had stopped at the same time as Lauda.)

The fact that Hunt—usually so decisive in switches to or from slicks—dithered was indicative of a racing (in a bad way) mind. He needed his hand held again. That the team didn't cotton on and issue an "In!"—a command rather than a recommendation—was indicative of its agitated state. The truth is that neither party "wanted to make the fucking decision." The prize was so close that they could smell the success and taste the fear.

First Patrick Depailler, who had not been wet-nursing his Tyrrell's sextet of tires, passed Hunt, quickly followed by the pole-sitting Lotus of Mario Andretti, who had been religiously fording puddles.

James did the math: Niki out; third good enough.

That became second when Depailler suffered a front puncture on lap 64 (of 72). Even less reason then for Hunt to risk a pit stop. Or more. His left-rear Goodyear had started to sag.

All concerned were relieved of this agony on lap 68 when his front-left tire finally succumbed to the tearing action of the long right-hand bend that funneled cars onto the straight. The McLaren, its Day-Glo livery streaked by mud, veered drunkenly into the pits, its driver giddy with rage. The five permitted mechanics worked a minor miracle: four tires in 27 seconds, once the nose, scraping on the ground because of the double puncture, had been manhandled onto the front jack. Their driver now needed to exhibit that same combination of strength of bone and mind. It wasn't looking good.

His remarkable season flashed before Hunt as he accelerated along the pit lane on sizzling slicks. He had driven flat out since January, for this? He neither knew his position nor his situation. And according to his whirling state, his team was squarely to blame.

OPPOSITE: Chief mechanic Howard "Hampton" Moore uses a brace and bit to drill holes in Hunt's visor in a bid to prevent it from misting in the damp conditions.

The new, improved Hunt had not driven old-style angry since qualifying at Interlagos. Now he cursed them all: probably Mayer at his most infuriating; those stupid scrutineers at Jarama and Monza—and, while he was at it, Snetterton; oh, and MaxfuckingMosley; and PatrickfuckingDepailler; the gods on Mount Fuji; the snobs at the RAC Club on Pall Mall; that bloke in Spain who had jogged his elbow and spilled his post-race orange juice, and whom he'd felt compelled to punch; and all the doubters.

His livid, vivid red mist, played out against a backdrop of a setting Oriental sun, hazed the pit signals that he passed and the cars he overtook. Cold stats on such an occasion were for cold drivers. Lauda might have made sense of them—had his airport-bound taxi not lost radio contact when it dipped in a tunnel.

Hunt had actually reemerged fifth, so widely spread were the remaining runners. The drivers he blithely breezed by in a single swoop around the outside of the track's slowest corner were Alan Jones in a Surtees and Regazzoni: men once fourth and third, who were now fifth and fourth. The latter might have put up more of a fight had his tires and career at Ferrari not been at their frayed edges.

Third was sufficient for his needs, but Hunt, ever more unsure, set off after Depailler. He was closing on the pesky Frenchie, too, when the checkered flag fell to greet Andretti, whose front tires were worn to the canvas, but whose Lotus was a lap ahead.

The slowing-down lap brought Hunt nicely to the boil. He was gonna strangle some people, starting with "The Wiener." The strange behavior of his "welcoming" team further enraged him. Already shouting and swearing, he scrabbled at the buckle of his helmet. He wanted the whole world to hear this.

And the whole world took a pace back when the volume of his tirade duly increased.

All, that is, except for the smallest guy on the scene. Mayer held his ground as Hunt, standing in the cockpit of the McLaren, towered and glowered. The same smile that James had spotted from a mile off in Germany now escaped him, even though it was mere feet away.

Nuance had no currency. Unable to make himself heard, never mind understood, Mayer thrust a three-fingered "victory" salute. Then a euphoric mechanic tore the number 11 decal from the pinging, clicking, cooling McLaren and symbolically ripped it in half.

His red mist lifting, Hunt paused.

"You're third, James. You've done it!" interjected Mayer.

- -

OPPOSITE (TOP): Hunt's admittedly small cup runneth over. As darkness descended, it finally dawned on him that no one was planning to take his world title from him. It had been that kind of season. **OPPOSITE (BOTTOM):** Hunt-san delights his fans. Female company was a motif of his extended stay in Japan.

CHAPTER 9

Jumbos and Budgies

James parked, appropriately enough, opposite the Tip-Top Bar, a CV joint on his Wolf WR7 broken after just four laps. He had begun his grand prix career in Monaco in 1973, and he had decided to end it here. And now. There was sentiment in his decision—although he paused for the first installment of his wages to be paid before announcing his retirement in June.

Six months later in Montreal, at one of his least favorite circuits, Niki hopped from Brabham's brand-new design, certain after only a handful of laps in practice that it would be a winner. He walked over to team boss Bernie Ecclestone, whom he had recently beaten in a seven-figure game of financial "chicken," to tell him that he didn't want to do Formula 1 anymore. They rescinded their contract for 1980 by mutual consent.

OPPOSITE: You'll have to speak into my good ear, James. Lauda and Hunt in 1977. **ABOVE:** Hunt oversees the charging of the trophy awarded for his 1977 British Grand Prix success. Joining him on the podium are a half-hidden Lauda, the runner-up, and Gunnar Nilsson. In front of a packed house at Silverstone, "rock star" Hunt worked his way through the pack after a dragging clutch caused his McLaren M26 to make a slow start from pole position. He harried leader John Watson for many laps before the latter's Brabham faltered because of fuel starvation. Nilsson might have caught Lauda's brake-less Ferrari had Lotus waved him by his hampered teammate Mario Andretti a few laps earlier than it did.

James had planned to let some time drift between **walks on a Spanish beach with his beloved Alsatian Oscar** and puffs on a J. But he soon got bored with the Costa living.

Whereas Hunt felt frightened and disillusioned, Lauda felt nothing—and that's what frightened him. There was, however, sentiment in his decision, too. The new car had a Cosworth instead of the Alfa Romeo flat-12 that had scuppered his two seasons with the team. It was a move sound on all fronts except sound. The V8's flat note failed to reverberate with Lauda. Illogically, "The Computer" missed the siren song that had been the aural backdrop to the best part—and best parts—of his F1 career.

He left to run a commercial airline.

Hunt ended up breeding and showing budgerigars.

James had planned to let some time drift between walks on a Spanish beach with his beloved Alsatian Oscar and puffs on a J. But he soon got bored with the Costa living and returned to England. He preferred tax to exile.

Niki, too, would chill at a Spanish villa, but only on the free days that his studied time-and-motion work schedule earned him.

James was trying to unwind. Niki was on fast-forward.

Hunt had been surprised and underwhelmed by the fleeting elation of becoming World Champion. In early January 1977, after a hectic two-month tour of glad-handing, promotions, and motor shows—including a rapturous reception in Bologna that discombobulated him—lunches with dignitaries and awards dinners—including a drunken scuffle at the RAC Club—he was both mentally and physically unprepared for the start of the new season in Argentina. He was still in the zone, as evinced by three consecutive poles, but he didn't feel energized like he had been in 1976. No matter that he had signed a much more lucrative contract with Marlboro Team McLaren.

Lauda, in contrast, was in 1977 as fired up—rather than motivated—as he had ever been, thanks to the detested presence of Carlos Reutemann, those contract-waving rows with Enzo, and the need to reconfirm his status as the Scuderia's leader. In his opinion, Ferrari had cost him the 1976 title, not vice versa, because of its "decision" not to apply team orders to Clay Regazzoni at Monza, and that broken suspension in Canada. Lauda simply considered Hunt to be "a helluva driver" who had beaten a better car fair and square.

- -

OPPOSITE: Wearing a typically provocative T-shirt, Hunt makes his way to the pits before the 1979 Monaco Grand Prix. He had already decided that he would retire from Formula 1 after this race.

Hunt's team boss Teddy Mayer insisted that his number one had given an "average car a helluva ride." And Hunt himself had no problem with how the title had been won. He had driven balls-out from beginning to end, and, when he applied his analytical side, reckoned that his misfortunes had been on a par with Niki's in terms of points lost.

Not everybody agreed with Lauda, Mayer, and Hunt.

Although those in the know raved about Hunt's performances in Canada and America, the uninformed majority's view was that he had taken advantage of a rival's near-death experience. Despite his bluster, this bothered Hunt, who had none of the constituent parts of the Lauda System to deal with it. Driving fast, as he was discovering, was no longer enough—in all respects.

The Lauda System, according to its creator, involved a check on your emotions; no fraternizing (except with Hunt, ironically); "a certain peasant cunning"; überpunctuality; a fast, businesslike mind; and short, no-nonsense answers. Niki was the boxer, James the puncher.

Lauda retook command of Ferrari in 1977 by undermining Reutemann's standing as a test driver: new front wing, fresh set of softs, splash of fuel, and—hey, presto!—half a second found inside half a dozen laps. Easy.

Carlos won the second round in Brazil. One month later, after intensive weeks of setup tweakery in Reutemann's absence, Niki won in South Africa and embarked on a run that was the very model of consistency in what was no longer the fastest car: 10 podiums that included three wins, six second places, and a third.

Hunt, meanwhile, couldn't stay out of trouble, steady a wobbling team, or provide it with a developmental focus. His tempered enthusiasm for testing had plunged to zero, and no amount of moaning by Mayer could alter that fact. McLaren should have drafted another driver to do the donkeywork with the recalcitrant M26, and released its rested thoroughbred at race weekends. Caldwell sees this now; at the time, however, he had donned a tie and moved upstairs to adopt an altered role at which, he admits, he was not as adept.

The dynamic of McLaren had shifted. It was no longer the best-organized team in the paddock. Once a fortress, it had become a glass cage, and Hunt, who had never seen eye to eye with Mayer—he was not alone in that, to be fair—would become less of a free spirit and more of a loose cannon.

OPPOSITE: Lauda leads Hunt (1), Carlos Reutemann (12), Mario Andretti (5), Hans-Joachim Stuck (8), Patrick Tambay (23), Jody Scheckter (20), Jacques Laffite (26), and the rest at the 1977 Austrian Grand Prix. The surprise eventual winner is the white Shadow DN8 of Australian Alan Jones, behind John Watson's Brabham (7) in this photograph. Hunt led the race in style until his "development" Cosworth V8 failed after 43 laps. With it went all realistic hope of successfully defending his world title.

The truth was that Lauda had been desperate to administer a slap in the face since **Enzo's emotionally stunted response** to his phone call from the Tokyo airport.

The M26 wasn't raced until round five in Spain, in May, and it wasn't as good as the venerable M23 until round 10 in Britain, in July, which is when Hunt scored his first win of the season, from pole position. He finished the year strongly with superb wins at Watkins Glen and Fuji, but fifth place in the points was poor reward for a driver who had set six pole positions and led 10 of the 16 grands prix.

At the height of his powers and popularity, Hunt was cockier than ever, and had become the objectionable person he feared he might in the circumstances. His behavior reached a new low in Canada when, after losing a hard-won and very brief lead because of a misunderstanding with Jochen Mass, he floored a marshal. "Hunt the Punch" also slighted the Japanese by skipping the podium ceremony at Fuji to dash for a plane. Worried about forfeiting personal freedoms, he cranked up his whims, caprices, rages, sulks, and eccentricities, and tended to play to the audience. And he always had an audience. This, of course, encouraged the non-motor-racing media to become more intrusive, and alienated the specialist press. Hunt reckoned the situation "worse than being at school." A boy's mind in a man's body, he was still his mum's "naughty James."

Lauda was behaving badly also. Fourth place at Watkins Glen in early October secured his second world title in three years. Having signed for Bernie Ecclestone's Brabham at the end of August—joining McLaren would have been too easy; he wanted difficulties to overcome—he walked away from Ferrari with two races still to run. He used the excuses of its planning to enter three cars in Canada and Japan, plus its sacking of chief mechanic Ermanno Cuoghi, who was following Lauda to Brabham. The truth was that Lauda had been desperate to administer a slap in the face since Enzo's emotionally stunted response to his phone call from the Tokyo airport. Theirs was an unfair fight—Enzo was 79, and unprepared for such hit-and-run tactics—and Lauda would later express remorse. It felt so good at the time, though.

A spoiled brat and "The Rat."

More easy-going Brabham was good for Lauda. Because he was under less scrutiny than he had been at Ferrari, he was relieved not to feel the need to be angry all the time. Hunt and McLaren, however, continued to slide in 1978: one podium finish, eight points, a handful of failures, and a host of incidents. Neither his M26 nor Lauda's Brabham BT46—except in its short-lived "fan car" B spec—was a match for the beautiful ground-effect Lotus 79, but it was obvious which driver was making the better fist. It wasn't "The Punch."

In Brazil, Hunt "simply lost interest and spun off." His race-terminating spin in Britain appeared so inept that rumors suggesting his off-track lifestyle was beginning to adversely affect his on-track performance began to gather pace. According to some friends, he would ingest harder drugs—cocaine and LSD—only if offered. But he was taking them.

Lauda barely touched the stuff. Any of it. He once shared a spliff with wife Marlene in 1984 and vowed "Never again!" after suffering a flashback to his Nürburgring fireball. He knew where to draw the line; Hunt did not. They went to the same parties on occasion, but it was Lauda who called it a night at a reasonable hour, and it was a hungover Hunt who would pull over and park his car by the side of the track for a snooze during the next day's test.

With mind-and-body guru Willi Dungl continuing to massage Lauda's muscles and mind, Niki had no need of artificial stimulants. Hunt, as his "dippers" increased their depth and regularity, felt he had nowhere else to go, nothing else to turn to. His spiral of depression, drugs, drink, and sleep deprivation tightened after he pulled Ronnie Peterson from the flaming wreck of a Lotus at Monza in 1978. More than his friend's subsequent unnecessary death due to medical complications, it was the look of fear in his eyes that seared Hunt's soul.

It didn't help James that he was labeled a hero for his actions. He didn't feel like one; he didn't want to be one. Near hysteria, he considered retiring from the sport there and then, but was

ABOVE: Lauda heads for retirement in the 1977 Argentinian Grand Prix at Buenos Aires. A malfunctioning fuel-metering unit caused his 312 T2 to gradually slip down the order before stopping for good on lap 20. The other Ferrari of Carlos Reutemann finished third. Asked before the race if he considered Reutemann to be a teammate or a rival, Lauda replied acidly: "Neither." Hunt started this race from pole position and was leading on lap 31 when his McLaren's rear suspension broke.

Hunt and Lauda see the funny side of their predicaments at the 1979 Argentinian Grand Prix, the season-opener in January. Both men suffered myriad problems with untested new designs during practice, and qualified only 18th and 23rd as a result. Hunt's debut race for Wolf ended after 41 laps when his WR7 suffered electrical problems. Lauda's race was hampered by a lack of fuel pressure in his Brabham's BT48, with Alfa Romeo's new V12 engine, and he called it a day after just eight stuttering laps.

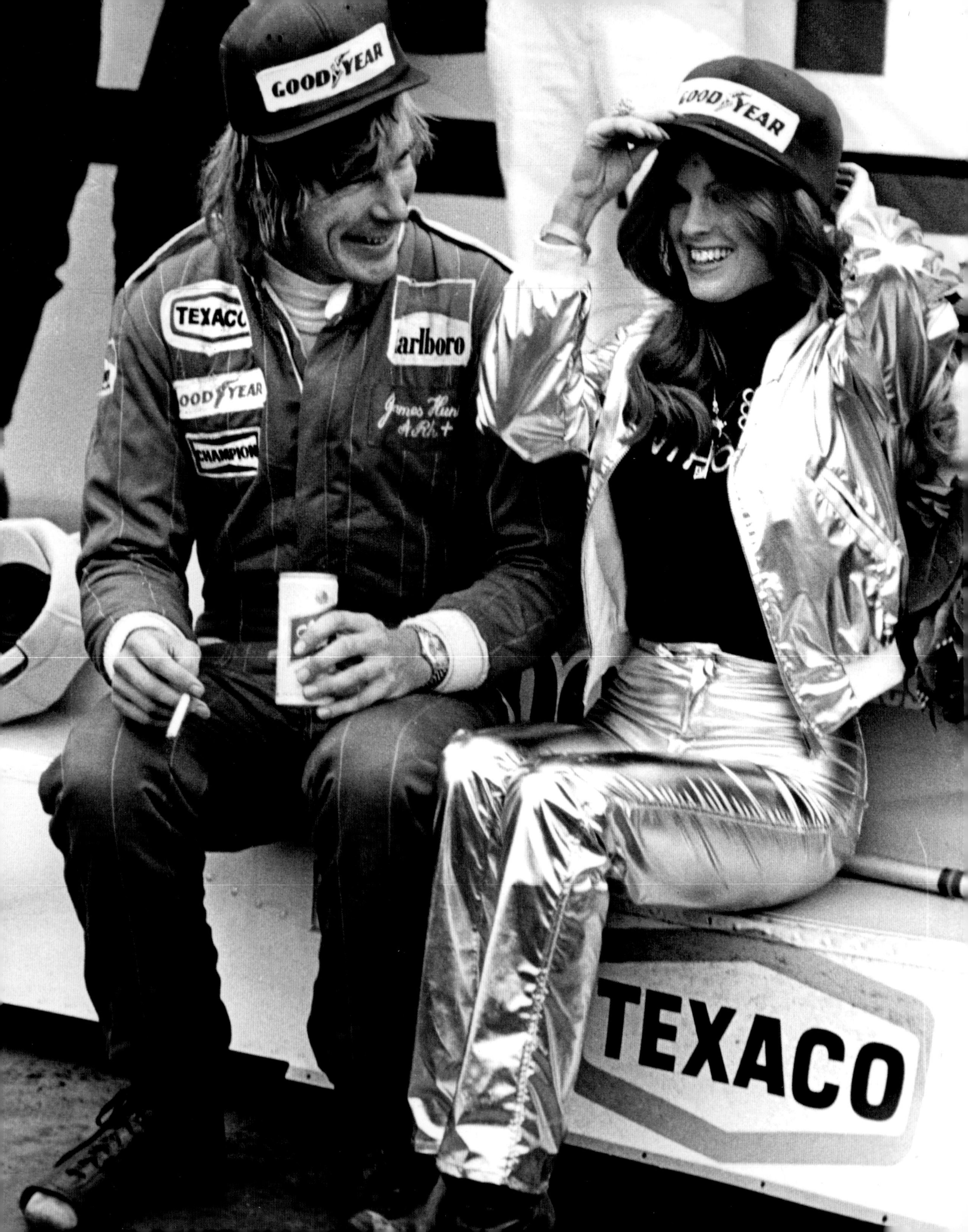
GOODYEAR
GOODYEAR
TEXACO
GOODYEAR
CHAMPION
TEXACO

talked out of it by Peter Warr and Harvey Postlethwaite, team manager and designer of Wolf Racing, for whom Hunt had signed for 1979.

They shouldn't have bothered. An increasingly nervy and darty Hunt, who had turned down a more lucrative offer from Ferrari in order to realign with his Hesketh mucker "Doc" Postlethwaite in a one-car team, was not much more than a disruptive influence. Cars WR7 and WR8 gave him reasons to be concerned—loose steering rack and brake caliper—and little cause for hope. The team had trouble coaxing him into the cockpit on occasion. Winning was the only thing that had ever brought him (temporary) peace of mind, and, with no chance of that at Wolf, Hunt was dazed and confused at 31.

Lauda was crystal clear about his reasons and intentions. Going around in small circles was stupid. He had bigger ideas to fly. He turned his back on the sport because his heart was no longer in it. Hunt turned away from the sport because his mind was cluttered. Although both men would miss the buzz and focus of motor racing, only Lauda had the spare capacity and drive to make a successful comeback.

Niki rediscovered his love for the sport in 1981, and forged a mega deal with Marlboro and the reconstituted McLaren for '82. He is adamant that money was not his motivation. He made an instant impact as the "shop steward" during a drivers' strike at Kyalami in January—and won his third race back. He would add another seven victories and a third world title to his tally before realizing—at Monaco in 1985—that he was in the wrong job, in the wrong place, at the wrong time. Though assailed by doubt for the first time, he stuck it out to the end of the season.

Hunt considered a one-off return with Williams as early as 1980, but all thoughts of this were kiboshed by a knee badly injured in a skiing tumble. The lingering pain this caused—it was worse than anything he had suffered in racing—soured him some more. His engagement to Jane "Hottie" Birbeck missed its moment, and James began to wonder if he was capable of experiencing genuine love.

In 1982, he met Sarah Lomax. They married in the December of the following year, called each other "Beast," and shared a Wimbledon house with their dogs, a tame robin, and an African Grey parrot with a blue vocabulary. There were wild parties, but equally they were for a time content with TV dinners and walks on the common. James also had his shrinking golf handicap, snooker table, and aviary—obsessions all—to keep him occupied. Meanwhile, the birth of sons Tom (in 1985) and Freddie 22 months later allowed him to exhibit his doting side.

Lauda also fathered two sons: Mathias (1979) and Lukas (1981). He admits that their arrival—he was midair for the first birth—affected neither his decisions to quit or to resume racing, nor his punishing schedule. He worked and stayed in Vienna, while his family lived near Salzburg.

OPPOSITE: Hello, my name is James, and I'm a racing driver. A *Penthouse* Pet receives Hunt's full attention after the 1977 US Grand Prix at Watkins Glen. The Englishman had been peerless in victory in the race's wet conditions, and dominated proceedings in his McLaren M26 after early leader Hans-Joachim Stuck crashed when his Brabham BT45B jumped out of gear at the first turn.

When James split from Sarah in 1988, he bought her and the boys a house around the corner. Ironically, it was their increasingly bitter divorce that snapped him out of "it." Although his worsening malaise had included more public urination—this time on a Boeing—and another scuffle—this time outside a low-rent Doncaster nightclub—he was becoming increasingly reclusive. Having to battle lawyers and face up to his financial losses with Lloyd's of London gave him much-needed impetus.

Falling in love helped, too.

Hunt was surprisingly shy and awkward to begin with, and could muster only regular coy visits to the local hamburger joint where Helen Dyson worked as a part-time waitress. It would require more than two years of careful and considerate wooing before this Fine Arts student agreed to move in with him.

During this period, James embraced a healthier lifestyle, some of which he would have dismissed only a few years earlier as hocus-pocus. His gas-guzzling, big old Merc on blocks in his drive, he cycled everywhere—when he wasn't driving his Austin A35 van in an uproarious manner. He still dressed like a scruff, but inwardly he was fit and happy. He even pondered a racing comeback, and tested a Williams for reference and research purposes in 1990—but he was several seconds per lap too late.

His rediscovered enthusiasm for the sport manifested itself in other ways: He mentored an appreciative future two-time World Champion, Mika Häkkinen, among others, and acted as an articulate and insightful consultant for teams. But the most obvious change was broadcast by his work with the BBC.

Since 1979, he had been teamed in the commentary box with Britain's "Voice of Motor Sport," Murray Walker. The latter, a fastidious and punctilious man who *had* attended Sandhurst, considered Hunt a "Hooray Henry," and was appalled by his slapdash approach to mass communication. This "chemistry" between them, however, was compelling from the off: Murray standing and shouting; Hunt laidback and laconic—except when he was flogging one of his hobbyhorses.

The most infamous of these was driver Riccardo Patrese, whom Hunt blamed for the Monza crash that led to Peterson's death. As well as instigating the young Italian's banning from the subsequent grand prix, he also provided a written deposition for the prosecution at the subsequent manslaughter court case. It was three long years before Patrese was absolved. Many felt Hunt was attempting to deflect the blame—his McLaren and Peterson's Lotus had provided the trigger touch. If he was, he had no need to. It was a racing accident caused by a chaotic starting procedure and flawed track layout.

- -

OPPOSITE: A young and delighted Ayrton Senna is clearly impressed by wily old fox Lauda's victory at Brands Hatch in 1984. This British Grand Prix was decided by the aggregate of two legs because of a race stoppage caused by Jonathan Palmer's crash in a RAM-Hart. Lauda was pressuring McLaren teammate Alain Prost for the lead when the latter's gearbox failed just beyond mid-distance. Britain's Derek Warwick (left) finished second for Renault, and Senna was third for Toleman. This was the latter's second podium visit in his first season of Formula 1.

Patrese never forgave him—but the more measured, in word and deed, Hunt earned the respect of many of those whom his behavior and attitude had embittered over the years. At last he was as comfortable in his own skin as Lauda had always been in his. Hunt said his friend and rival was the bravest person he had ever met—and a better human being since his accident. Lauda said his friend and rival was the most charismatic driver the sport had ever known, and that he had exhibited "unbelievable strength to get out of the shit." Mutual appreciation societies are not renowned for accurate character assessments; this one, however, was spot on.

Closer to home, Hunt made a tacit peace with his parents, a verbal peace with Sarah—and proposed to Helen. She accepted gladly, albeit via telephone because she was holidaying with girlfriends in the Aegean at the time.

Her phone rang again the next morning, this time with bad news: James had died of a massive heart attack. He was 45.

In August 1976, the world had waited with bated breath for word of Lauda. Expected to die, he had lived; such was his spirit.

On June 15, 1993, the world had to come to terms with the sudden and unexpected death of a man whose spirit had waned on occasion, but who had by his own endeavor eventually given himself every reason to live.

The brave are not always favored by fortune.

A reunited Lauda and Hunt chew the fat in the dilapidated pits at Monza in 1981. Hunt was working for the BBC, whereas Lauda was there as a spectator. Ostensibly. In fact, he had driven to Italy to speak with Ron Dennis of Marlboro McLaren International about the possibility of a future secret test of a Formula 1 car. Lauda had the itch again. The graffiti behind his head proved prophetic: He would win again at Monza. His victory with McLaren at the 1984 Italian Grand Prix was his fifth and final win of a season that saw him become the World Champion for a third time.